READY

THINKING

READY

THINKING

PRIMED FOR CHANGE

5 PRINCIPLES FOR ACTION
IN TIMES OF UNCERTAINTY

JOHN BAKER

Wonsockon Publishers
Eden Prairie, Minnesota

Published by
Wonsockon Publishers
Minneapolis, MN 55347

Publisher's Cataloging-in-Publication Data
Baker, John.

    Ready thinking : primed for change / John Baker. — Minneapolis, Minn. : Wonsockon Publishers, 2008.

    p. ; cm.

    ISBN: 978-0-9818852-0-9

    1. Organizational behavior. 2. Management. 3. Leadership. I. Title.

HD58.7 .B35 2008
302.35—dc22   2008932088

Interior design by Brooke Camfield
Project coordination by Jenkins Group, Inc
www.BookPublishing.com

Printed in the United States of America
12 11 10 09 08 • 5 4 3 2 1

Contents

Exercises

Disclaimer

Everything in this book is true. Actually, that's not the truth. *Most* of the stories and examples I use in this book are true. Those that are not true are, in general, accurate. I have taken the liberty to refabricate the timing and recombine the order of things to make a salient point. With this in mind, everything in this book is *truthful*. Hopefully, you get the point.

The people whom I quote and whose experiences I relate in the book are real. Names may or may not have been changed based on my discretion as to whether the anecdote I was relating was a complimentary reflection of someone or whether it made that person look like a nitwit. I have fudged a bit around titles and blurred the lines of organizational structures to avoid having certain leaders or coworkers (some of whom I had the pleasure of working with for many years) come off as complete idiots. They weren't.

The sage says that when the wise man points to the moon, the fool looks at the finger.

I'm shooting for the moon.

Acknowledgments

All contents of this book are original. Actually, this statement is not true. Trust me: there is nothing in this book that you have not read, heard, or thought of before. Paul Johnson, author of *Creators*, writes, "All creative individuals build on the works of their predecessors. No one creates in vacuo." I certainly agree—although I am only guessing at the exact meaning of the word "vacuo."

My source material includes two decades of successfully leading thousands of people in America's largest companies, in rough-and-tumble industries, in good times and bad. I have a liberal arts education, an MBA indoctrination, and access to the Internet, magazines, and various "thought of the day" desktop calendars. You'd be amazed at how READY Thinking concepts are echoed throughout the universe in different forms and fashions.

The writings of Anthony de Mello are a clear and undeniable source. His book *Awareness* is a life changer. For many years, I have encouraged people to read his work. This book shows how his messages coalesced for me as I struggled to be a good person and a strong leader in my own life.

As de Mello would say, take it or leave it. I'll be fine either way. So will you.

chapter 1

The READY Thinker

"Leaders accomplish things that reach beyond their solitary abilities by acting—and getting others to act— with a maturity that surpasses limited self-interest."

Personally, I'm not really into reading books on leadership. But I keep wondering why certain people act consistently strong during times of inconsistency, why some remain resilient despite negative odds, and why some emerge victorious while others succumb to pressure. I keep questioning how a leader can bring out these behaviors sometimes but not all the time.

Most of us lead in some way: at work, at home, at school, as a coach, or wherever you hold influence over others. Leaders make a difference, good or bad. The framework of thinking I outline in this book can provide you and your entire team with a method to get motivated and prosper.

I call this new framework of thinking READY Thinking.

READY Thinking is what successful people use, consciously or subconsciously, to effectively take action in the face of both challenge and opportunity. READY Thinking allows an individual to get motivated, to tackle tough problems, to flourish in times of turmoil, to move through change more rapidly, and to win more often.

Perhaps you've noticed that some people are more capable of staying motivated than others. They're better able to deal with the change they confront. These are individuals who grasp opportunity more ably and consistently move through times of stress. They attract energy and followers. They are action oriented, moving forward with confidence and purpose.

Then again, perhaps you've observed others equally affected by circumstance who are left paralyzed and diminished by change. These are the miserable ones, mired in self-defeating thoughts and inaction. Caught leaning back on their heels, these folks seem to miss opportunity when it knocks and grumble about the hand that life has dealt them.

I developed READY Thinking in the real-world laboratory of some of America's largest corporations. I have firsthand experience in leading thousands of employees and challenging them to avail themselves of change and seize opportunity. Frankly, some could, and some couldn't. I have been intrigued by those who could, individuals who seem to win consistently in life. They tend to have a unique approach to living, a style of intellectual toughness, and an emotional suppleness that enables them to achieve their goals and ambitions, often in the face of disturbing times.

Great leaders throughout history, as well as the great spiritual and intellectual thinkers throughout time, all speak of a type of thinking that infuses the soul with peace, courage, purpose, and bearing. Privilege and adversity strike indiscriminately, but those who face them using certain core beliefs and thought patterns motivate themselves to win and succeed.

This book is intended to introduce you to the concepts of READY Thinking and teach you how to apply them to heighten your personal mastery, increase your own performance, and intensify the impact you have when leading and influencing others.

So let's get started with the basics. What is a leader?

I have no idea. Don't look to this book to tell you. I am as mystified as the next person by what a leader is.

Frankly, "leadership" strikes me as a rather ticklish thing, a hit-or-miss proposition. Even great leaders have blotchy leadership complexions. Abraham Lincoln, by most accounts, didn't have much success in life, and then he became arguably our country's finest president. As mayor of New York City, Rudy Giuliani was seriously grating on the nerves of his constituents on September 10, but 9/11 became a day that defined his character as a leader. One might argue that St. Peter, a disciple of Jesus Christ's who went on to build the Christian church, scored a tad low on the leadership curve during the early-morning hours of that first Easter weekend, when he denied three times even knowing Jesus. Winston Churchill acted like a deadbeat brother-in-law—a hard-drinking, cigar-smoking, get-up-at-noon kind of guy who bums money and raids your refrigerator—before becoming a hard-drinking, cigar-smoking, get-up-at-noon kind of guy who took down Hitler and the Nazis and was instrumental in saving the free world.

Apparently, no one has a perfect record. There is no serum to inject. Rather, leadership is a method of thinking that, once adopted, leads to certain productive action.

So, while I don't know what a leader is, I know what good leaders do: **Leaders accomplish things that reach beyond their solitary abilities by acting—and getting others to act—with a maturity that surpasses limited self-interest.**

I sweated over that line. I wanted it to be of impact. I even put it in bold for you. I want to grab you right here in Chapter One. Get a marker and highlight it. I think it is very good.

And that's not all! I give you license to use that line, anytime and anywhere you'd like. Quote it in your next meeting. Use it in an upcoming presentation. Work it into a conversation. Integrate it into your résumé. Go ahead—knock yourself out.

But, do so with one very important thing in mind. Like every other leadership bromide, others will use this one too: good people, bad people, good leaders, bad leaders. You can teach that line to a parrot, but it won't make it a leader.

This is why it is helpful to think of leadership not as a thing but as a course of action, not as something you talk about but as something you do. READY Thinking is about adopting a posture that precipitates action. It is practicing a method of thinking to set you up to be influential during change, to move through obstacles, and to size up and grasp opportunity.

Eerily, the worst leaders often talk the best game. Like some kind of paranormal phenomenon, those least inclined to take action are often the ones who say the perfect thing—especially in a group setting.

The. Absolute. Perfect. Thing.

Uncanny!

This isn't leadership. Don't be fooled. This is no more than a horn player who plays notes but can't create music.

I am reminded of the epitaph written by the Earl of Rochester over the death of Charles II:

Here lies our mutton-eating king,
Whose word no man relies on,
Who never said a foolish thing,
Nor ever did a wise one.

Some people talk a good game, but **in the crucible moments when true leadership is demanded, theirs finds no purchase**.

I like that line too, so I put it in bold.

READY Thinking is a framework of thinking that produces influential action, a method of bringing revolutionary thinking into places where leadership is required. It uses the simple acronym READY to encompass the following five principles:

R is for **R**eality: Defining the situation in uncompromisingly clear and concise terms for yourself and the people around you. It is the most essential step in READY Thinking—and the hardest. This book will explore the great secret of reality and four key barriers that stop us from defining it.

E is for Enlarging: Giving yourself and those you lead an aspirational, energy-inducing vision much larger than the task at hand and much bolder than the situation warrants.

A is for **A**ccountability: Authentically taking responsibility for your actions and the leadership you give to others. Most important, you'll learn when not to be accountable. That's right: in READY Thinking, you'll learn about the value of not being accountable!

D is for **D**urability: Persisting through tough times, finishing the job, and valuing the benefit of sweat and toil. Learning about the privilege of suffering a setback.

Y is for a **YES!** Outlook: Having a YES! Outlook on life means looking at change as a chance for growth. It is the practice of asking "What can I do with this change?" as a first reaction, rather than "What will this change do to me?" Having a YES! Outlook means taking what you do seriously but not taking who you are seriously. Life's pretty short! Why not laugh and enjoy it?

These five principles can have tremendous impact on both your life and the lives of those you lead.

Are you READY?

chapter 2

The Difference between Management Thinking and READY Thinking

"Reason is God's shadow."

Can you be a leader without being a manager? Sure, but it's a risky thing, akin to tackling a soufflé without knowing how to separate egg whites. It shows pluck but lacks prudence. In truth, being a good manager is an essential part of leadership. Leadership is grounded in the discipline of management. But thinking as a manager and thinking as a leader are two entirely different things. READY Thinking is about being a leader.

Let's keep things simple. In life, there are things you know and things you don't know. Managers spend considerable amounts of time and energy on getting as many things transferred from the unknown into the known.

To do this, managers rely on experience, education, communication, and observation. They measure, weigh, gauge, and test inputs to determine likely outcomes. They instill disciplined controls to make sure that processes remain consistent and repeatable. The good ones are never complacent. They strive to calibrate performance levels to tighter allowances. They are erudite and thoughtful, most often boring and droll. Hey, but that's what you want in a good manager: someone who can grind it out and limit any "bad" surprises. That's why you don't see DVDs being sold over the Internet with the title *Managers Gone Wild—Spring Break!*

I proudly claim to be manager—and a good one at that. I have the tattoo to prove it.

Our need to manage our world and bring control out of chaos is instinctive and dates to the time of creation. The book of Genesis outlines God's work to create heaven and earth:

> *In the beginning God created the heavens and the earth. The earth was without form and void, and darkness was upon the face of the deep . . .*

Before creation, there was no shape to anything. Complete emptiness. Nothing. Zip. Nada. *St. Thomas Aquinas walks into a bar and says to the bartender, "What did God do before he created heaven and earth? Nothing. He didn't have time!"*

In seven days, God brings forth order and goodness from the void and empty space by creating light and dark, sky and water, land and vegetation, the cosmos, birds, fish, animals, and man. When you consider the work involved just to get your kids out the door to catch the school bus, this seems *très omnipotent.*

Ancient Greeks studied the stars to manage activity around a propitious phase of the moon or to avoid an ominous omen of a planet. Pythagoras, he of the tormenting theorem, and his followers searched for the existence of some controlling principle underlying the apparent randomness of the universe back around 500 BC. (His theorem, some claim, was discovered etched centuries beforehand on a Babylonian tablet circa 1900–1600 BC, but, alas, it was quickly forgotten by Babylon High students.) Aristotle wrote perhaps the first précis on the science of management:

> *Excellence is an art won by training and habituation. We do not act rightly because we have virtue or excellence, but we rather have those because we have acted rightly. We are what we repeatedly do. Excellence, then, is not an act but a habit.*

Management is the process of controlling things.

Management is the discipline of anticipating and limiting life's variability, best suited to define the present condition and illuminate a credible path to a likely future. In a perfect world, our control over things would have us contend with nothing but foregone conclusions.

But, our world isn't perfect.

No matter how much you know.

No matter how much you've sweat the details.

No matter how well you've isolated the variables.

No matter how in control you think you are.

There are always things you do not know.

There are always things you cannot know.

This is where leadership is required.

Nothing succeeds quite as you planned. The discipline of management is not to be confused with authority over life. The business model isn't reality. Even our most concerted efforts in time management can't control time.

Life is funny. Sometimes it comes at us like a manic, cocaine-fueled, hyperkinetic, frenzied Robin Williams. It's not concerned with "getting to yes." Change smacks our seven habits upside the head. Crisis thumps our power of purpose. Chaos knocks us on our cans, stands over us, and taunts us like a schoolyard bully. *You think you're the master of your Day-Timer?*

So we are compromised, caught between our drive to control things and the realization that not everything can be controlled. The irony of our situation was not lost on the mystics. The call to quell our yearning for certainty and relax our compulsion for answers is ancient. Rumi, the celebrated thirteenth-century Sufi poet, beautifully wrote in *The Masnavi*:

> *Sell your cleverness and buy bewilderment. Cleverness is mere opinion, bewilderment intuition . . . Reason is God's shadow; God is the sun. What power has the shadow before the sun?*

Reason is God's shadow. What gifts are our intellect and our ability to think, reason, and understand. What a joy our senses. They give us the ability to gain insight and perception and discern information about the environment surrounding us. They are wonderful and empowering, but they do have limits.

Despite our best efforts, we cannot explain away all the uncertainty in life. We cannot predict all outcomes. Something larger than ourselves operates outside of our rule. St. Paul, in 1 Corinthians, writes:

> *It is written, eye hath not seen, nor ear heard, the things that God has prepared for them that love Him . . . The natural man receives not the things of God.*

Other books can give you the blueprint for how to think like a manager. In this book, you'll be learning how to think like a leader. You'll learn how to flourish when things don't go as planned, to press forward when the chips are down, to face a disrupted and disorderly environment and have the courage to pierce through the fear of the unknown and achieve success. Life has a bad habit of interrupting our carefully laid plans. Winning people, and winning organizations, are those who get through these periods of uncertainty more quickly.

The first step is realizing the difference between management thinking and READY Thinking.

chapter 3

What Does It Feel Like to Be READY?

"Enchanted by the possible."

D o you want to be fully alive? To savor the whole gumbo of life—certainty and ambiguity, planfulness and spontaneity, deliberation and impetuosity—with confidence and determination?

Do you want to hear life's whole orchestra? To have the capacity to know life's nuanced music? To achieve copability, not just capability, and adaptability, not just preparedness? Not just be able but durable?

That is what READY Thinking can deliver.

During the course of this book, I am going to ask you to participate in various "Two-Minute Drills." These are short, simple, experiential exercises that you can complete, generally, without having to get up from your chair.

Two-Minute Drills require that you quiet yourself. Clear your head of your dominating mental chatter. Give your brain a time-out. Relax. Your goal is to have no goal. Just sit and be absorbed in the moment. This is tough stuff for you A-types. Your mind is like a snow globe that you've been vigorously shaking for years. *Stop it!* Your swirling thoughts are coloring your perceptions. Once your mental snow has settled, calmness and serenity can emerge. You become able to bring a relaxed and focused concentration to the exercise. Insight comes from an added clarity in your thinking and a heightened keenness of attention.

Dog-ear this page, because throughout this book, I will ask you to prepare for Two-Minute Drills by taking the following steps:

1. Eliminate as much external distraction as possible. Turn off your Blackberry. Don't look at your e-mail. Put your phone on "call forward." You don't need absolute quiet, but taking as much external noise out of the equation as possible will help with the process of calming your mind. You can easily conduct these exercises on the train or bus, at the kitchen table, or in your office cubicle.

2. Sit up straight. Place both feet flat on the floor. Rest your arms loosely on your thighs. If you'd like, you can close your eyes, or keep them open if you prefer. If they remain open, try to avoid watching the clock, or who is walking by, or scores flashing on ESPN, etc. If you close your eyes, don't go to sleep.

3. Take a big breath in. Hold it for a few moments. Then expel it outward. Relax and release the tension in your muscles. Start at the top of your head and concentrate on the tension in your body. Concentrate on the feelings you have on your scalp. Breathe in and out. Relax. Concentrate on your forehead. Breathe in and out. Relax. Move slowly down to your face, neck, and shoulders. Each time, feel the tension in that specific body part and concentrate on releasing it. Continue through your whole body, down to your legs,

feet, heels, and toes. Try not to *think* about this process of feeling. Just become aware of the feeling and experience the sensation.

4. Thoughts, memories, emotions, and daydreams will pass through your mind and may disrupt your meditation. Become aware of them and resist the urge to focus on or judge them. Detach from them. See them as clouds passing before the sun. Let them drift by. Gently move back to your body sensations.

5. Do this for as long as you feel comfortable. Five minutes is fine. Ten is great. At first, this type of self-observation might feel awkward and perhaps a tad embarrassing. With greater frequency comes both familiarity and practical benefit.

Using the above steps, prepare for the following Two-Minute Drill:

TWO-MINUTE DRILL
HOW DOES READY FEEL?

Consider a time in your life when you felt completely ready, a time when you had done all you could to manage a situation by identifying and controlling as many variables as you could possibly foresee. Yet, an experience where the future was far from certain, the outcomes unknown, the risks high, and the emotions flowing. It was a moment for which you felt completely—perhaps strangely, surprisingly—prepared to face. Maybe it was:

- an important scholastic test or an important job interview
- a presentation you made to an important investor or board of directors
- a sales pitch to a whale of a prospect that could make or break your year

continues ➤

- a concert or theatrical performance or keynote speech
- a sporting event with seconds on the clock and the game on the line
- a wedding proposal or wedding day or meeting the in-laws
- a difficult conversation with a contemporary or relative
- the birth of a child
- the death of a loved one

Whatever the situation, mentally take yourself back to this event. How did you feel? (And, please, don't say, "I felt ready.") How did "ready" feel? Emotionally, what was going through you? Physically, how did your body react? How did others perceive you? How did you perceive others? What were you thinking?

Consider this experience and jot down your thoughts to the following prompts:

The situation was _____

I remember feeling _____

I remember thinking _____

I was aware of _____

The experience gave me a sense of _____

When describing it to others, I'd say _____

To think of it now reminds me of _____

This is an exercise that I ask seminar attendees to complete. I ask them to recall a situation in their lives when they were on the threshold of something suddenly new and unpredictable, a situation when they had trained or studied, one when they felt they could exercise at least some control beforehand yet could not completely anticipate all the outcomes. Still, standing on the verge, they felt "ready."

In providing me feedback, they say things such as:

- "I felt confident. A little worried but not overly so. Certainly not to the point of paralysis. I was excited to get on with the change."
- "I remember thinking how calm I felt. Chaos seemed to be raging, but I could emotionally distance myself from it and keep perspective. I was aware of the drama but wasn't part of it."
- "The game slowed down. I saw the playing field more clearly. I didn't notice the crowd noise. I was in the zone. I called for the ball. I wanted to take the shot."
- "I felt on the balls of my feet, able to quickly respond. I was intent on taking action. I was moving forward, not ignorant of the risks, but I was moving forward in the face of the risks."
- "The mistake in the performance came without warning. I just reacted. I didn't think about it; I just improvised. It was only later that I thought about the mistake and how I had extemporaneously dealt with it. The composure I had felt was amazing. It was an exhilarating feeling."
- "I felt that I was processing information and getting to meaning more quickly. I connected the dots. I wasn't feeding information through my traditional mental filters but was far more mentally agile. I felt like I was using the entirety of my brain."

After going through this exercise, one person described the feeling as "enchanted by the possible." Isn't that delightful?

Is there a place in your leadership—at work, at home, in your marriage, as a parent—where these types of reactions would be beneficial? To get people excited in the face of change? To get them motivated and willing to move forward without complete clarity of information? To respond quickly, to "want the ball," to seek out action? To be composed and confident in times of turmoil? Nervous without being paralyzed? Exhilarated by potential?

I remember the day when my wife, Tammy, told me that she was pregnant with our first child.

Surprised? Not completely. Scared? Freaked beyond recognition. Excited? Spinning out of control like the Tasmanian devil. We immediately began to secure as much information and manage as many variables as possible.

Tammy reassessed her diet and began eating better foods. We attended Lamaze classes. She sized me up as her delivery coach and then asked the doctor what pain medications were available.

We explored the hospital and toured the maternity wing. We saw and touched all the gadgets that were going to be plugged into and around Tammy. I diagrammed the route to the ER, analyzed alternatives through the city, and highlighted side streets and shortcuts. We set up the nursery and purchased enough diapers to handle all the bowel movements from all the babies in the five-county area.

We got outfitted: a crib built by an Amish guy, a changing stand, the Humvee of strollers, a baby bounce-up, two-way monitoring systems, mobiles of pink and blue fish, bunny curtains, dollies, soft blankets.

Tammy's belly got bigger. She'd drop a spoon, and some old crone in the restaurant would tell her she was going to have a girl. She carried low, which meant a boy. She had terrible heartburn, which meant the baby had a lot of hair. In the early morning hours, the weight of the baby would press on her intestines, kinking them like a garden hose and prohibiting her from sleeping. I would rub her back, and we would talk about our fears. We talked. We listened. We planned.

At Tammy's final prenatal checkup, the doctor assured her that it would be at least another two weeks before the delivery. That same night, her water broke, and she embarked straight into severe contractions two minutes apart.

Her: "My water broke."
Me: "No, Tammy, you must be wrong. Are you sure you didn't just pee the bed?"
Her: "Steady, *Cool Hand*, get the car. It's go time."

And at that moment, we were no longer in control. Something greater than us was in control. Our son, Jack, as it turns out, not yet born, was completely in control.

All the work, the planning, the learning: over. Where were the faintly uncomfortable eight-minute-apart contractions that we had been promised? The mild tummy twinges? The slow, steady, calculated buildup of manageable labor? The *"Not to worry, honey, we have time"* spasms?

Our planning had been impeccable, our preparations like D-day. But, the moment Tammy's water broke, we realized that our coping skills would now be as important as our organizational skills.

How did we feel? Exultant! It was the moment we had been waiting for: unpredictable, scary, emotionally overwhelming. We were ready and raring to go, nervous but on high alert. We were eager to move forward. We acquiesced to the internal conflict of seemingly incompatible emotions. **We felt reconciled to act.**

Are you able to recall how it feels to be "ready"? To know the stakes are high yet—paradoxically—feel no oppressive tension? To feel nervous but confident, calm but energized? Feeling clear-sighted and on your toes? Feeling likely to do your very best?

You felt READY.

Whereas management is establishing control over things, READY Thinking is effectively influencing through things not under your control.

Being ready is a joy. Feeling unready is miserable. Being ready is being confident, calm, nimble, and proactive; being unready can be humbling, humiliating, frustrating, and embarrassing. Imagine if we could get ourselves and the people we lead to stand before change and think differently and be ready.

That's the goal of this book: to allow us to become better people and better leaders by learning how to influence through those uncontrolled or uncontrollable factors affecting us and our performance. This requires challenging some timeworn leadership assumptions and sacred cows. By providing for ourselves and the people we lead a different framework for how to think—how to engage in READY Thinking—imagine the potential impact we can have, especially in those groups, families, and organizations going through discordant change. What would it be worth for you to move through this change faster, seize opportunity, eliminate delay and foot-dragging, and overcome obstacles and the shockwaves they cause? And to do so with a resolute and committed team?

It might be worth learning what READY Thinking is all about.

MICHELANGELO WAS A READY THINKER

Consider Michelangelo's brilliant statue of David, the boy king of the Bible. A 17-foot-tall symbol of victory. Victory of enlightenment over darkness, reason over fear, action over hopeless paralysis. David is the magnificent representation of the READY Thinker.

The statue *David* stands boldly in Galleria dell'Accademia in Florence, Italy, the birthplace of the Renaissance. A young Michelangelo carved it from a whole block of discarded marble considered so large and useless that it had earned its own nickname: *Il Gigante*. Michelangelo captures David at the very moment he sizes up his enemy, Goliath.

Look into *David's* eyes: he is alert and aware. Notice his posture. Despite the risk, he stands relaxed and confident. He has quieted his mind and is poised to do battle. His countenance is attentive and beautifully self-assured.

Across the battlefield, no doubt, stands Goliath: a brute possessing enormous strength. One can almost imagine Goliath shouting insults and scornfully mocking the young boy he is facing. Goliath is a barbarian, and for 40 days, he single-handedly defied the armies of Israel. "Is this the best you can do? Is this your greatest warrior?" His contempt for David would drip from him like sweat.

David stands audaciously naked, wearing no armor, confronting the giant with only his wits and body. His weapon of choice is unconventional: in one hand a stone, in the other a rudimentary slingshot.

Goliath, one can envision, is terrifying to behold: a monster standing over nine feet tall, enfolded in armor and brandishing enormous weapons. All who gaze on him are paralyzed with fear—all but David. Where others see only indefatigable malice, David sees opportunity. Goliath's head is hideously large, nearly as big as David's whole body, and it is a fearsome thing to look at. David, in his composure, sizes it up as a target. The Bible story

continues ➤

goes on to describe David's ultimate victory. His stone flies true from its sling, and he slays Goliath.

For Michelangelo, Goliath represented more than the threatening Philistine of the Bible story. Goliath was the perfect symbol of the uncivilized, chaotic, and dark days of the Middle Ages that enlightened Florentines struggled to transcend during the early sixteenth century.

A 26-year-old Michelangelo was commissioned to sculpt a statue to adorn the top of the Duomo of Florence. The Florentines would not have it. They adored *David* so much that the statue was displayed in the Palazzo Vecchio, the town center. It became the symbol for their Renaissance city: a forward-looking island of achievement, enlightenment, and optimism triumphing in a sea of dark and destructive forces.

chapter 4

The R in READY
Thinking: Reality

"When the archer shoots for nothing,
he has all his power."

Napoleon said that the first priority of a leader is to "define reality." Fair enough but far easier said than done. It's like trying to grab a handful of water: seems to be something you'd be equipped to accomplish, but, splash away as you might, it often leaves you frustrated and wet.

It is more accurate to say that defining reality is the ***most difficult*** thing a leader has to accomplish.

Without a doubt.

Why so difficult?

Here's a secret: very few people like reality.

Governing your life is about choosing, but the old adage is true: people want their cake and eat it too. When leaders take the time to define reality, they do so at their own peril.

Anthony de Mello, in his book Awareness, uses the metaphor of being asleep: it's unpleasant for people to wake up. They won't appreciate your efforts to get them out of a warm, cozy bed into a cold room.

Prepare for a Two-Minute Drill. (Remember, to prepare, go back to the page you dog-eared in Chapter Three.) Take a few minutes to get your mind in a position to gain value out of this work.

TWO-MINUTE DRILL

ASSESSING REALITY

Consider the following:

Would you rather be told you are good at what you do?

or

Would you rather be good at what you do?

This exercise has three possible answers.

First, some people claim that there is no difference between the two choices. These people are off their meds. There is a world of difference.

Second, some people admit that they would rather *be told* they are good at what they do, even at the expense of actually being good. As cynical as these attitudes seem, they are, in a way, refreshing. You know where you stand with these folks. They're as abrasive as sandpaper, but at least they've come clean and are being honest with you and with themselves.

The third answer, the one most people land on, is that if you had to choose—which, regrettably you do, since it's part of the drill—you would rather be good at what you do, even if you weren't recognized for it.

This might be stretching reality a bit.

Prepare for a Two-Minute Drill.

TWO-MINUTE DRILL

ATTACHMENTS

Think of something to which you are very attached, something you have strived for and accomplished, something that demonstrates your achievement.

- Your corner office
- Your professional designations and awards
- Your title, salary level, bonus program, long-terms, etc.
- Your bank account or balance in your 401(k)
- Your reputation
- The respect of your peers
- The Beemer
- The Florida condo
- Your country club membership

Pick one of these things or something you thought of and consider the amount of hard work you expended and how much time you spent to attain it. Now, say to this thing, "I do not need you to be happy. I could lose you tomorrow and still be fine. The joy in my life is not dependent on having you. I can do without you. My happiness and sense of fulfillment are unburdened by an attachment to you."

How easy is it for you to say these things?

Do you believe yourself when you say them?

continues ➤

> What emotions do you feel as you "let go" of the attachment you identified in the exercise?
>
> What fear do you observe in yourself as you say these powerful words?

The challenge of saying "I'd rather be good at what I do than be told I'm good at what I do" is the reality that we really like being told we're good at what we do. Often, the rewards and recognitions associated with what we do *are* the reasons for what we do: they are the things that make us happy.

The reality is that attaching our happiness to things makes us dependent on them. We fear their loss. We develop a need not unlike a craving. Our things start making demands on us. In difficult and uncertain times, we fail to lead because we sense inordinate risk: our sense of well-being is threatened.

When you feel threatened, the hypothalamus area of your brain revs like a muscle car. Hormones secrete, and the nervous system engages. Adrenaline and cortisol hit the bloodstream like a fuel injection. It's fight-or-flight time, the same response our ancestors had when bursting out of the blocks to avoid being shish-kebabbed by a sabertooth. While the stress level in our culture is less man-eating, it is more unrelenting. Constant change to our environment, uncertainty, chaos—and the high levels of associated stress—mean we never hit the hypothalamus "off" button. Our fight-or-flight reactions become unremitting, resulting in the inability to cope with trivial matters of the day and generating excessive amounts of cortisol and—if the infomercials are true—stubborn belly fat. Prolonged levels of cortisol in the bloodstream can impair cognitive skills, increase blood pressure, lower immunity, and put you in an early grave. We overreact. We lose sight of what is important. We easily panic and become prone to paralysis. We hit the brakes and look behind us when we should be stepping on the gas and moving forward.

Imagine the power you would have—the speed with which you could act, the clarity of thought and immediacy of engagement—if you were able to be indifferent to the rewards and recognitions to which you have attached value in your life.

Peter was someone who joined a large corporation after successfully building a small technology consulting firm. Peter spoke often about how exhilarating it was to build a successful technology business, how winning in an industry filled with big egos and oversupplied with cutthroat and unscrupulous competitors was fine fare. It required long hours, he would say, countless miles traveling on the road, and a lot of street smarts.

But it had its rewards.

Peter wore suits tailored in London, drove a Ferrari, and lived in an exclusive neighborhood in a mansion that sat magnificently atop a hill that rolled gently down to a breathtaking lakeshore. His boathouse looked like Graceland.

Later it was learned that most of what Peter represented about himself was exaggerated. His small tech company wasn't the uber-firm that he portrayed. It had struggled, like most start-ups, to get off the ground. Facing liquidation, Peter had sold his stake and took a job in the marketing department of large conglomerate in part for the stability that the company offered. His wealth, as it turned out, had been inherited. He wasn't successful by the benchmarks that he himself professed.

During the short time Peter worked for the large company, he never came off of his story. He continued to boast about being a successful entrepreneur while struggling to adapt to the corporate culture. He neglected to network within the organization and turned cynical with delays and the bureaucracy. That is, until the day he was asked to leave. He was more interested in promoting his reputation as an entrepreneur than he was in being good at what he was doing. His grasp on his "toy" was so tight he couldn't let go.

Peter wasn't willing to face reality.

What were the leaders at Enron focused on when they led their company into bankruptcy? *Being good at what they did?* What about the leaders at Arthur Andersen, WorldCom, Global Crossing, and Tyco? What about the corporate executives who backdated their stock options? What about the ones who overstated sales figures, overextended into risky markets, downplayed excess inventory levels, or used "creative" accounting to cover cracks in their balance sheet?

The leaders of these organizations were smart, competent people. They were accomplished. They had charisma and prowess. Yet, somewhere along the line, their judgment became contaminated. They became self-indulgent. They became addicted to the glory of having people tell them that they were good at what they did and forgot—or chose to ignore—the reality of their situation.

Chaing Tsu, a fifth-century Taoist, wrote:

> *When the archer shoots for nothing, he has all his power.*
> *When he shoots for a brass buckle, he is already nervous.*
> *When he shoots for a prize of gold,*
> *He goes blind, or sees two targets.*
> *His skill has not changed, but the prize divides him.*
> *He cares.*
> *He thinks more of winning than of shooting.*
> *And the need to win drains him of power.*

Prepare for a Two-Minute Drill.

TWO-MINUTE DRILL

POWER OF INFLUENCE

Consider the line in Chaing Tsu's poem, "When the archer shoots for nothing, he has all his power."

Think of a time in your life when you felt powerful. Not from a position-power point of view or from having "authority" over someone or something—rather a situation where you truly felt instrumental in being able to influence a person, a group, a situation, or an outcome.

What is the situation? _____

_____

_____

How did "having all your power" feel (and don't say "powerful")?

_____

_____

_____

Why were you able to feel this way? What was at stake? Who was judging you?

_____

_____

Great influence often comes in situations where you have no particular meritorious endgame in mind, nothing specific to gain or lose. As such, you are free and open to go with the flow. You clearly hear what others have to say and are judicious in your own comments. You're above it all. "Take my advice or not," you say. "I am indifferent."

Prepare for a Two-Minute Drill.

Two-Minute Drill
Situational Response

You probably have one example in your life where you were very good at something and went unrecognized for it or where you were the best candidate for a job, a choice assignment, or a promotion but were passed over. Think about this situation. How did this make you feel? What emotions were you experiencing?

_____

_____

_____

_____

You also probably have one example in your life where you undeservingly achieved a goal—perhaps by luck or by association—that truly wasn't your accomplishment but you were awarded and praised nonetheless. Think about this situation. How did this make you feel? What emotions were you experiencing?

_____

_____

_____

_____

Which situation felt better to you?

_____

_____

_____

_____

Once in while, you bump into people who haven't followed a traditional path and are busy doing their own thing. Mike dropped out of the corporate world in order to paint with a vision all his own, indifferent to any commercial value of his work. Does he want to sell paintings? Sure, but not at the cost to his vision and passion. Annette is on staff at a nonprofit organization. She could make more money and gain more accolades in the public sector, but she chooses to follow a different set of rules.

When you see this healthy indifference to self-glorification, you are lucky: you have met a true craftsperson. Craftspeople are those who work to a standard that they themselves have set. They are both relatively uninterested in your opinion of them and unconcerned whether you validate their work. They would prefer that you think positively of the work they do, but your approval is not the thing they aim for. Their yardstick of success is in the purpose of the work itself.

HAL IS A READY THINKER

Hal was a carpenter recommended by a friend. My friend noted that Hal had been working for a large construction firm but had recently decided to strike out on his own as an independent contractor. My friend said that since Hal was just starting out on his own, he needed the business.

"That tree branch hit my house," I said to Hal as I pointed to the huge limb laying in the yard, "and my roof has a hole in it."

"Here's the deal, though," I continued after a long moment. "I'm getting ready to sell this house. I was hoping you could do a quick patch job on it. Make sure that the roof doesn't leak, but at the same time, do the work quickly and keep the costs down. I won't be living here much longer, so if the shingles don't exactly match or if you use scrap to fix the fascia, that's okay by me. You can just bend that crumpled gutter back into a semblance of its original shape and tack it back up there. No one will know the difference."

Hal looked at me and then looked at the house. "I can't do that," he said, shaking his head. "I'll know the difference."

"Don't get me wrong," I said, taken aback. "I'm not asking you do anything illegal. Just save me a few bucks by cutting some corners. I can't tell you how many corners the previous owner cut. He plumbed the dishwasher using electrical conduit. He wired the bathroom with stereo cord. You should see the fuse box: it looks like it's grown dreadlocks. It really is a wonder that the whole house hasn't burned down."

Hal said, "Well, it was nice meeting you." He started walking back to his truck.

"You see," I said following behind him, "I was hoping to get this job done quickly. I thought you could use the business."

"I could use the business," Hal said over his shoulder. "It's tough starting out. See you later."

"Wait, Hal," I said dumbfounded. "Is this job too small for you? What would it take for you to give me a bid?"

Hal leaned on his truck.

"John, this job is not too small. I'm willing to get started on it tonight, but I'm going to do it right. When I went out on my own, I decided that I wouldn't cut corners and that I was done doing things half-baked. The Yellow Pages are full of guys who would be glad to take this job. I don't work that way. I'll fix that roof the right way and charge you a fair price. When the new owners of this house look at the roof a year from now, or 10 years from now, they won't be saying the same things you said of the previous owners."

Would you hire Hal? And, when a neighbor needed his porch rebuilt, or a friend wanted a deck added to her house, or a coworker needed bathroom remodel, whom would you recommend?

Like all craftspeople, Hal awoke one day in a traditional job and said, "I can do better than this." He decided to free himself from the roller coaster of seeking the approval of others. He took the brakes off of his life. He wasn't controlled by an addiction to praise; his actions were uncontaminated by the need to please others.

Mother Teresa Was
a READY Thinker

By common benchmarks, Mother Teresa was an acute under-achiever. Many of the people to whom she ministered died in her care. Not good for a nun's year-end performance appraisal. Despite this, she won the 1979 Nobel Peace Prize; she has been beatified by the Vatican; and her Missionaries of Charity, the Roman Catholic order she started in 1950, has attracted thousands of members worldwide.

Mother Teresa worked with the poorest of the poor. She was known as the "saint of the gutter." In her ministry, she would seek out the desolate and desperate, those souls who were literally within hours of death and beyond help, people without hope. It wasn't a cure that Mother Teresa was looking to provide but a sense of grace. She would take these miserable, filthy, and decrepit human beings and bathe them, clothe them, feed them, and lay them down on a soft bed—all so that these people would find kindness and charity in the final moments of their lives, so that they could see the love of God if only for a brief moment before their death.

Can you imagine doing this for a living? How could Mother Teresa accomplish this? What in the world motivated her to get out of bed in the morning, day after day, and face this challenge? Well, she's a saint (or one step away) for starters. But, she also thought about her life this way:

People are often unreasonable,
illogical, and self-centered;
Forgive them anyway.

If you are kind, people may accuse
you of selfish, ulterior motives;
Be kind anyway.

If you are successful, you will win some
false friends and true enemies;
Succeed anyway.

If you are honest and frank,
people will cheat you;
Be honest and frank anyway.

What you spend years building someone
could destroy overnight;
Build anyway.

If you find serenity and happiness,
they may be jealous;
Be happy anyway.

The good you do today people
will forget tomorrow;
Do good anyway.

Give the world the best you have
and it may never be enough;
Give the world the best you've got anyway.

You see, in the final analysis,
it is about you and God.
It was never about you and them anyway.

In many different ways, leaders can have their attention drawn away from reality; it can be ugly and unpleasant, can conflict with outcomes we desire, and can threaten the things that we perceive make us happy. Naturally, under such conditions, our behavior becomes tenuous and uncertain. We think of what's at stake, and we hesitate. Our attention becomes divided.

READY Thinkers focus on reality by finding that presence deep inside, sometimes called a higher power, to accomplish things with love and purpose.

chapter 5

The First Barrier
to Reality: Labels

"The unobserved life is not worth living."

The world around us has too much information. There's no new news in that. What is new is our bottomless access. Managing unconstrained contact with information is like trying to pour the ocean into a hole in the sand.

I do a lot with my PDA, but I could do more—so too with my word-processing software, computer, phone, digital camera, satellite TV, wrist-watch, toothbrush, and iPod. But, I don't. Like most people, I use what is essential or, more accurately, what I have had the time to learn.

The term for this is "technological compression." We are in the Age of Proximity. Everything, everywhere, is at our fingertips. Want to see recent rock music from Prague? No problem. How about finding that missing Hummel? E-Bay to the rescue. Want to know what's going on in the French Quarter? Dial up the OysterCam.

It is the image of technology as a supreme Zeus, granting us all our wishes from his pinnacle on Olympus. But, equally valid, it is the image of the multiheaded Hydra. We glory in the ability to condense our world onto our laptops, all the while fighting new and multifaceted pressures that come along with this demonic power. To tame the monster requires slicing through the never-ending regeneration of information.

Managers must concede to the power of technological compression. Life, and the work we do in it, is fast paced, and decisions are expected with only a moment's consideration. Technology has made for an influx of information that is simply too great to absorb. To avoid the loony bin, we have to decipher. Goal achievement requires a high degree of selectivity. Our senses are bombarded by stimuli, some relevant to the task and some not. Attention has to be allocated and reallocated to often competing definitions of success. There isn't time to methodically understand and translate all there is to know. We have to place our bets very quickly. Categorizing incoming information through the use of labels helps accomplish this.

Labels allow the species to survive. If we waited until all facts were known, we'd make better decisions, but the decisive moment would be long gone. Given enough of this, we would surely become extinct. While good managers insist on getting as much ambiguity boiled out of a situation as possible, there are strikingly few sure cinches. At some point, you have to suck it up and make a decision.

Ever work for managers who can't label? It's exhausting. They never make a decision. Their mental gears spin, twirl, and rotate, but nothing comes from it. You hear the machinery hum, but they drive you mad with calls for more information and more data. They value reasoning and logic over action and results. But, in life, whether at work or at home, results are (surprisingly often) called for, and so managers have to *decide*. Managers must use the discipline of labels to define things that they cannot exhaustively classify or fully understand in order to make an actionable decision.

And once they do, they lose understanding of what it is they are managing.

How's that for a paradox?

Prepare for a Two-Minute Drill.

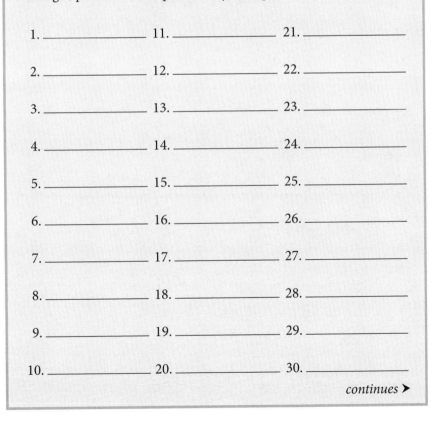

TWO-MINUTE DRILL

PERSONAL LABELS

In the next two minutes, write as many one-word labels as you can think of that you would use to describe yourself. Think about labels that would describe you both at work and personally. For example: manager, processor, salesperson, shy, tall, quiet.

1. _____	11. _____	21. _____
2. _____	12. _____	22. _____
3. _____	13. _____	23. _____
4. _____	14. _____	24. _____
5. _____	15. _____	25. _____
6. _____	16. _____	26. _____
7. _____	17. _____	27. _____
8. _____	18. _____	28. _____
9. _____	19. _____	29. _____
10. _____	20. _____	30. _____

continues ➤

Step 2. Because people don't have time to learn everything about you (Don't be so full of yourself!) cross out every item after 7. While you're at it, cross out items 1 through 4: many people won't believe who you say you are simply based on face value. Finally, if today's date ends in an odd number, cross out 5 and circle the description of yourself that you have written in 6. If today's date ends in an even number, do the opposite: cross out 6 and circle 5.

In the space below, write, in bold letters, the word you have circled.

Hello, I'm:

Step 3. Imagine placing this name tag on your lapel and walking around introducing yourself with this label for an entire day. Imagine introducing yourself to people you meet, and imagine them responding, "Oh, so you're _____." How would it make you feel? Do you think it is a fair assessment of you? If someone you met saw this name tag, do you feel it would give him or her an accurate or complete sense of who you are? Would you rather have used a different label? Which one? Why?

When I do this exercise during my seminars, I hear an audible gasp as I winnow the list. No one likes to have his or her first label eliminated, let alone the first four or five. *They're the best ones.* Nor do they like to have such an arbitrary process employed for the final selection.

I then have the seminar attendees actually fill out name tags and place them on their lapels and ask that they spend five minutes circulating around the room simply introducing themselves with this one and only label.

The feedback I get is enlightening, from "It was great" (the one who had "Stud" down as his choice) to more common responses such as "It felt narrow and confining." "Unfair." "Silly." "Embarrassing." "Misleading."

I often take a moment to randomly read a few select labels from the various name tags around the room.

"Team member?" I'll shout. "I need another team member like a punch in the face! There is too much consensus building around here. Stop meeting with each other and get something done!"

"Quiet? I don't need quiet people. I want people who can speak up and get results."

"Friendly? What kind of brownnoser are you?"

"Results oriented? Just what I need, another stressed-out, type A employee eager to grab all the credit."

You can see where this is going.

"That's not me," folks will mutter. "I'm quiet, but I speak up when I need to."

"Where do you get off?" they say. "I get results *through* teamwork."

"Time-out! I am not just one thing," they protest. "I cannot be pigeonholed into one label. Trying to put who I am or what I do—let alone what I am capable of doing—into one category is far too limiting and doesn't allow you to understand who I truly am."

Once you label something, understanding stops. Labels allow you to manage but stop you from seeing full reality. They are shorthand, nothing more or less.

In *War and Peace*, Tolstoy wrote, "In historical events great men—so called—are but the labels that serve to give a name to an event, and like labels, they have the least possible connection to the event."

Unattended, our labels are preconceived notions that pretty much lead us where they will. Unchecked, our labels can do more to define how we experience life than our senses do.

Prepare for a Two-Minute Drill.

TWO-MINUTE DRILL
UNATTENDED LABELS

Take a look at the list of words below. These are words that describe a person who, for purposes of this exercise, you just met. After reading the description, write down the words that describe your first response or impression.

Slouches _____

Lisps _____

Blond Hair _____

Male with Ponytail _____

Obese _____

Southern Accent _____

Middle Eastern Accent _____

Effete _____

Muscled _____

Bad Teeth _____

Tattooed _____

Low-Cut Blouse _____

Pierced Tongue _____

Step 2. Consider why you responded the way you did. Since you are predisposed to a certain way of thinking—based on your upbringing, your education, your personality, the friends you surround yourself with, your victories and failures, where you've traveled, what you have been exposed to, and what you have experienced—consider where these responses came from.

For example, if you responded "Looks lazy" to the word "slouches," you might say that this response came from your upbringing. Maybe your parents pestered you to sit up straight at the dinner table. Perhaps you have a background in dance or theater, where proper body carriage is an important part of your craft. For each response above, write where you think that response originated.

Making decisions using certain labels is clearly taboo. You may not discriminate based on the color of someone's skin or his or her ethnicity, age, gender, or sexual preference.

Other types of labels are more obtuse. On the face of it, it seems the height of common sense that we would steer clear of using labels that make us unhappy or prove ineffective in our lives. Yet, at times, we don't (or can't) avoid them. Why is that?

Here is a story that might help answer that question, and it involves my dad, Big Don. As a traveling salesman, Big Don spent his day driving from small town to small town as he tried to drum up business. During the day, his car was more than his mode of transportation; it was his private office, a mini-warehouse, his break room, his closet, his entertainment center, and his pride and joy. He kept his vehicle so spotless you could eat off the engine block. He liked his cars large, tricked out with all the options, and propelled by titanic horsepower.

He did not like anyone else in his car, for this upset the automotive eco-system and introduced nasty viruses into his pristine atmosphere. He had long ago abandoned his abode and all its rooms to an overwhelming tide of kids' crap. He put up with the lack of privacy and accepted that he might never again experience the joy of solitude in his own home.

But his car was different. His car was his castle, his realm, his only refuge. There he retained the role of the alpha male, energetically marking his territory and ferociously protecting its borders. In this environment, the wife was an annoying intrusion, and the kids—messy and disrespectful—were downright loathsome.

As such, we learned never, *ever*, to soil his territory. Since we were a one-car family, this made life interesting. Riding in his car was as delicate and tricky as a high-wire act. Upon entering, we sat as still as coma victims to avoid sullying the carpet or crushing the nap of the velour. We knew better than to drop a candy wrapper on the floor or, God forbid, bring anything into the car that was in liquid form. If you didn't like what was on the radio, well, your best bet was to shut up about it. Big Don wasn't the least bit interested in your opinion. You want the window open? Well, shut up. Cigarette smoke getting to you? Well, shut up.

One time, when the clan had all been loaded up and was driving down the road, Big Don decided to crank the heater to maximum. Despite the winter weather, the temperature in the car became as hot as the flame on a welder's torch. Dressed in our winter clothes, we sat crowbarred together in the backseat sauna, sweating like Eskimos in the tropics and breathing through our cupped hands in order to cool the air before it could singe our lungs. It was hot enough to soften the plastic on the armrests; the snow melted on the sides of the street as we drove by. Finally, Mom, at the end of her tolerance, reached over to turn down the heat.

Dad slapped her hand.

Oh. Yes. He. Did.

Despite the equatorial temperatures in the car, things turned very icy very abruptly. If anyone asks whether you can hold your breath while driving between the Twin Cities of Minneapolis and St. Paul, the answer is "yes." My siblings and I did it in 1973.

My shrink, Dr. Friedman, knows there is more to that story, but, tempting as it is to linger in the fertile garden of my adolescence, let's not. Rather, fast-forward to my first date with my wife-to-be, Tammy. I was ferociously smitten with her, a condition for which I have found, to this day, no cure. I open the car door, and she gets in. I go around, get in the car, and fire up the four cylinders. She reaches over to turn down the radio.

I slap her hand.

Somewhere a phonograph needle scratches across a vinyl LP. A cupboard full of china crashes over. Brakes squeal. The flux capacitor warps space and dimension. Time stops.

In truth, I didn't.

But, I almost did. It was my first reaction. What was I thinking?

Clearly, it wasn't in my best interest to slap Tammy's hand. A nice hand smack infuses doubt into any relationship and dramatically reduces the likelihood of a second date. I was confronted by a label that wasn't even mine: it was Big Don's! I always abhorred Don's "Lord of the Ford" behavior, and there I was copying it!

The reason we use certain labels, even when they don't work for us, is because we don't even realize we're using them. Labels operate like an "attentional blink," a proven phenomenon that links human attention (what we attend to) to human consciousness (what we are aware of). Behavioral scientists studying this phenomenon explore why some stimuli that strike the retinas in our eyeballs never get captured by our brains. When experiencing an attentional blink, humans seem to suffer a millisecond of amnesia.

Attentional blinks happen in a micro-instant and function as cognitive mechanisms that our brain uses in order to eliminate distracting stimuli. Much like the participants in attentional blink studies who could not perceive certain target letters streamed to them, our labels are such a part of us that we lack perception of them. We are so unaware that we vehemently deny that they even exist. As such, we fail to attend to them. Over time, we can identify with a label so strongly that when it is confronted, we feel the same emotions as if we had been physically attacked.

Prepare for a Two-Minute Drill.

TWO-MINUTE DRILL
PERSONAL IDENTIFICATION

Ask yourself this question: with what do you most identify your leadership? Is it a process? A technique or habit? A certain educational discipline? A reputation, a brand, or an image? A level of historical performance? A certain style? Or something else?

_____

_____

How would you respond if someone asked you, "What kind of leader are you?"

_____

_____

What books would you recommend on the subject?

_____

_____

What type of education or degree would you advocate?

_____

_____

What types of jobs are your skills and experience most suited for?

_____

_____

How firmly do you identify with your self-image as a leader? The tighter your identification is, the less likely you are to shed your labels and face reality. Consider the passion you bring to your role as a leader. Could you change to adapt to new facts, new methods, new information?

_____

_____

Peter Senge once said, "People don't resist change; they resist being changed." To change, people need to both recognize the value of experience and deprogram themselves from their labels they adopted during those experiences.

Winners do this.

What concepts and labels do you cling to? What do you identify with? Can you imagine the power you would bring to your life if you stopped adhering to preconceptions and demanding that your way was the only way? What would happen to you if you were open to new, unfamiliar ideas, ready for what came next?

When people cling to their labels, very little changes. But, when labels are dropped—whether in the business world or sports, science, or the arts—breakthrough thinking occurs.

Disney saw castles when others saw orange groves. Saulk found cures in the spores of everyday mold. Copernicus looked to the heavens and reasoned that the sun, not the earth, was at the center of the solar system. Darwin saw something revolutionary in flightless beetles. Dick Fosbury saw a high bar and flopped over it—*backward*. Mohammed Ali purposely took a thumping but reclaimed his heavyweight crown by rope-a-doping the unassailable George Foreman (before his grilling days) in the "Rumble in the Jungle." Twain cruised the Mississippi and found a true and uniquely American literary voice. Oppenheimer couldn't see the atom but somehow split it. Some daring soul ate the first oyster. Only when Ray Charles stopped singing like Nat King Cole did he become an American icon.

Continuous improvement (a management discipline) improves processes at the center of a system, an entity, or an organism; innovation (a leadership discipline) lies on the periphery, on the outer edges. You can't innovate if you simply stare at the core.

As leaders, we have to be the innovators, even in the face of criticism. Can we be nimble enough to adopt new strategies by letting go of the labels we place on ourselves and others? It is apparently harder than it seems

LOUIS REARD WAS
A READY THINKER

Louis Reard was a mechanical engineer by training but decided to become a clothing designer after he noticed female sunbathers on the beaches in St. Tropez rolling up their swimwear in order to maximize the amount of skin exposed to the sun. In 1946, Reard created a two-piece bathing suit so scandalous for the times that respectable fashion models refused to be seen in the belly-button-baring design. Reard resorted to hiring a nude dancer from the Casino de Paris to showcase his skimpy swimsuit. *Voila*: the bikini—"smaller than the smallest bathing suit in the world"— was created. This was just three weeks after the United States conducted atomic bomb tests on the tiny atoll in the Marshall Islands. It is unknown which event generated a bigger explosion.

because even our most exalted business leaders, the CEOs, fail at an inordinately high rate. How does someone who has worked so effectively to climb the corporate ladder fail when getting the top job?

These people become too tied to their labels. The CEO label clouds their memories. It's their way or the highway. They fail to recognize that their success is a reflection of the collective toil of many people. As CEOs, they recall that they did it all on their own.

The allegory is that of a dog leashed to a tree. Fido runs around the tree's trunk, and for a while, life is pretty good. He has enough slack to run over and sniff at something in the garden, then to dig a hole by the picnic table, and then to find his bone and bury it under the porch. Ineluctably, the leash starts wrapping itself around the tree trunk. Now, instead of the freedom of exploring the whole yard, little by little the dog's dominion gets condensed. His ability to roam is progressively limited until only a foot of leash separates him and the tree. Then, of course, all he has to experience is the tree, and he is bewildered; he can't quite figure out why he isn't running around the yard as freely as he once was.

Excuse the graceless metaphor, but to hammer the point home, you're the dog, and the tree is the labels you are leashed to.

In the world of marketing, there is something called an "endowment effect." This concept is the premise that consumers place more value on products they own or a service they use—a car, a type of coffee, a travel Web site—relative to products and services they do not own or use, even when the products and services are comparable in every way. What is so extraordinary about this is that consumers bend seemingly inviolate rules of economics by inefficiently placing a premium on a good or service that is indistinguishable from an alternative. The consumers penalize themselves by personalizing their attachment to the label on the bottle, or the shoe, or the tube of toothpaste.

What can you do to break your bond with coercive labels? Be prepared to "slaughter your innocents." In and of themselves, your labels and biases have done nothing wrong and have probably served you well. But, they are also the very things that cause you fear and attachment and make you hesitate when on the threshold of opportunity. READY Thinkers actively observe how labels that have worked in the past impact decisions today.

The Buddha said, "The unobserved life is not worth living."

Can you lead a full life without knowing what controls you?

Get rid of the labels and you'll be the CEO of your life.

chapter 6

The Second Barrier to Reality: The "What If" Game

"Life can only be understood looking backwards, but it must be lived forward."

Ilearned a great lesson in the Dallas Marriott hotel at 6:30 in the morning while I was getting out of the shower, buck naked and dripping wet.

I was in Dallas to do two things. First, I was there to calm down a client who was greatly upset with my company. Second, I was there to begin a quick weight-loss diet. Since the client was going to chew my butt off, I was pleased that I had a chance to accomplish both of my goals in one meeting.

My firm had been very slow to respond to changing market demands and had a long history of missed standards and chronic underperformance. Our products had been vilified in the trade press. Competitors were tearing us apart.

Why had it been so difficult for certain senior leaders to see how quickly we were falling behind in the market? They should have taken notice of our clients' increasing dissatisfaction. Sales figures had plummeted, and rebid indicators suggested lagging marketplace interest. Why had our firm been so obstinate in staying the course?

Like an old man getting out of bed on a cold morning, my company responded with strategies designed to correct the situation, but it looked to be too little too late. We were months—check that, years—behind. If only the development team had been more focused on what clients were asking for.

One good story, a lone positive statistic, one modicum of success, an iota of hope: anything would have provided me with precious air cover. As it was, I felt I was going into this client battle buck naked—which, a fleeting look in the mirror confirmed, I was.

The television in my hotel room was tuned to a morning network talk show. The guests being interviewed were Heather Whitestone, the newly crowned Miss America, and her mother, Daphne. Heather was the first Miss America with a disability: she has been profoundly deaf since she was 18 months old.

The morning talk show personality, let's call her Hannah Happyface, was wide awake, amped up, and in top form. She was asking penetrating questions such as "What was it like growing up deaf?" and "Did you ever think you'd be Miss America?" Heather somehow controlled her fist and answered each question with the pluck, poise, and patience of, well, Miss America. Meanwhile, her mother looked on and nodded in support.

Turning to Heather's mother, Hannah asked, "Daphne, I know you have a beautiful, successful daughter, but hearing the news of Heather's deafness and raising a nonhearing child had to be very difficult. Did you ever ask yourself, 'What if she hadn't been deaf?'"

In a calm voice and a no-nonsense tone, Daphne Gray replied, "Well, to begin with, we don't play the 'what if' game in our family."

Huh?

"We don't play the 'what-if' game . . . "

Like a thunderbolt, I realized how Heather Whitestone had become Miss America.

There had been no wasted time on useless "what if" games in that family, no needless distractions, no morbid fascination with fictional scenarios, no unnecessary wallowing, no allowances for feeling sorry for oneself.

The unexpected news of Heather's deafness had to have been calamitous and heartbreaking. In some families, maybe most, it would have proven catastrophic. But, for the Whitestones, the anguish of the deafness had been put behind them. They had found the strength to move on.

I sat on the edge of the bed and reflected on the power of that answer. Here I was, away from my home and family, once again in another indistinct location, preoccupied with things that weren't real.

What if I had a better product to support?

What if the product had performed better?

What if the firm's senior leaders had made different decisions?

What if there were more resources?

What if I had the product line that my competitors had?

What if there hadn't been any processing errors?

What if my technology was bug free?

What if? What if? What if?

What if my cat could bark?

What if I could use the "Force" to float the TV remote over to me?

Would I ever leave my easy chair?

I realized that I was spending big-time tuition bills to MSU: Making Stuff Up. I could work up creative alternative endings like a Hollywood screenwriter. If only I could go back in time and change history. I'd be Superman, flying around the globe at an impossible speed, reversing the rotation of the earth, turning back the clock, resetting reality, reworking inputs, and facing new, less discouraging facts.

I determined to stop playing "what if" games.

I drove over to the client's office (dressed nattily, I might add) and was escorted into the company's boardroom, where the contract committee was meeting. My main contact at the company, I'll call him Ted, greeted me at the door like I was his long-lost brother.

"How's the family?" Ted asked, shaking my hand and slapping me on my back. "It's been too long. Gosh, you look good. Any problems with your flight? The golf game okay? How 'bout them Vikings?" His countenance was so sincere that I thought he was going to plant a smooch on my buttock.

Ted motioned for me to sit at one end of the boardroom table, which was long enough to land fighter jets. He took the chair at the other end of the table. He was so far away it was like looking at him through reversed binoculars. Quiet as monks, other committee members shuffled in and took their seats.

Here's how Ted began the meeting:

"I want the minutes of this meeting to reflect how deeply disappointed I am with John and his firm. I am a patient man, but they have consistently not delivered on basic promises, and I am at the end of my rope. Their technology is not just inadequate but downright appalling. Their product performance is atrocious. I believe they are incompetent at what they do."

Ted's small talk was apparently over.

"I have recommended to this committee that we immediately terminate our contract and take our business to another provider. Your competition, by the way, seems very eager to take our business." He paused to let the drama of that statement sink in and then let out a dejected sigh. "However, in light of the fact that you have been a service provider to us for several years, this committee has asked that I give you the courtesy of explaining yourself prior to a vote on this matter."

The committee members all turned their heads toward me like I was that night's dinner. Did the lady three down on the left just lick her lips?

The room was as silent as a church. I knew I had about five ticks worth of time to save this account. Here is what I said:

"I agree with your recommendation, Ted. We deserve to be fired. Much of what has happened could have and should have been avoided. But, the fact is it wasn't. To go into it again and give you another round of explanations and excuses would be playing the 'what if' game, and I am done playing the 'what if' game. You have to make a decision that, everything being equal, you would prefer not to have to make. For this, I apologize. I am sure this committee has better ways to spend its time."

I paused and breathed in and out again. Ted hadn't moved. The coven batted nary a warted eyelid.

"I can see why you think that our team members are incompetent. They will be embarrassed to hear that you have this opinion of them. They don't show up to work in the morning wanting to be incompetent. What they want is to be great at what they do. And, they want to be great at what they do *for you*. Suffice it to say that they will want to do whatever they can to change your mind.

"At one point in time, not all that long ago, you compared us to the competition, and we won. We've let you down. We know that. There will be no 'what if' excuses, because we need to move forward. I can express a renewed commitment to this market on behalf of my firm. We are committed to improving our products' performance. Maybe it's too little too late, but if you choose to delay your decision and give us a grace period, you'll soon know. And, in the interim, you will benefit from our sincere commitment to regain your trust and confidence."

I stopped speaking.

After a long pause, Ted asked, "Is that it, John? Is that all you have to say?"

I nodded and stood up. "Yes, you know the rest," I said. "I want to keep you as a client. Not wasting your time is about all I can offer. Looking back, there is no reason for us to continue to work together. Nothing I can say will change that. Looking forward, though, I think we have a real opportunity to, once again, get on the right track and work well together. I sincerely hope you give us the opportunity."

Later, Ted called and said the committee voted to give my firm another six months. We were going to get another shot at proving that our improvement strategies would pay off and that we could right the ship. Ted was exasperated when he told me this news.

"There wasn't any reason to keep you guys around," he said. "The committee members thought you were honest and forthright, and they saw a renewed forward-looking energy that you demonstrated. They appreciated that you did not waste their time with more excuses and other such nonsense. Nothing personal, John, but you still deserve to get fired, and my vote was to replace you. The committee, though, thought you deserved one more chance. Don't blow it."

Prepare for a Two-Minute Drill.

TWO-MINUTE DRILL
THE WHAT IF GAME

Recall a recent situation when you played the "what if" game by using one of the following phrases:

- What if . . .
- If only . . .
- Would have . . .
- Could have . . .
- Should have . . .
- In hindsight . . .

Imagine that you have a rubber band on your wrist. Visualize yourself stretching the rubber band fully to its maximum elasticity. Now imagine letting the rubber band go and having it deliver a nasty snap to your innocent wrist. *SNAP!* Welcome to the "what if" game.

Now consider giving all the members of your team a rubber band and challenging them to snap it whenever the "what if" game is played.

During my seminars, I hand out a rubber bracelet with "GET READY" embossed on it. Participants put this "BMD," or behavior-modification device, on their wrist and then complete the drill above, snapping each time the magical "what if" game words are announced.

As of late, I have begun to hand out two such bracelets. Here's why. I bumped into Renee, an attendee of one of my READY Thinking seminars, at a coffee shop. She told me this story.

RENEE IS A READY THINKER

"I recently learned that my mother has breast cancer. My aunt was very distraught by the news and said to me, 'Your mother was never really one to take care of herself. She didn't go to the doctor and never had routine checkups. I don't think she ever learned how to do a self-examination of her breast. I can't help but wonder what if she would have checked and found the lump earlier?'

"At that time, I was still wearing my 'GET READY' wristband. I took it off of my wrist and put it on my aunt's. I told her, 'Mom really needs us right now. We can't waste our energy by playing the "what if" game. In order to take care of her, we have to accept her situation as it is.'"

Once you are in tune with the "what if" game, once you recognize it in all its glorious manifestations, you will not believe how much time you have wasted. You will begin recognizing how much work can get done in the space of time others are still working through "what if" mind games.

Don't confuse this discussion with the vital management practice of sensitivity analysis, packaging "what if" scenarios together in order to better understand how sensitive business metrics, such as budgets, sales goals, or performance targets, are to various stimuli. This is a best practice and an essential tool for good management. But, the key is in how such exercises are used: to forecast or help plan, not to rehash or remunerate.

"What if" games looking backward are invariably unproductive because they move us away from the reality of the moment. Soren Kierkegaard said, "Life can only be understood looking backwards, but it must be lived forward." You can't live life backward. You may seek understanding from past experience and perhaps learn a lesson along the way, but you have to apply these to your life moving forward. READY Thinking is about being out front and forging ahead.

Gossip and rumor are sophisticated "what if" games. Certain people relish the opportunity to rewrite the present by representing hearsay as fact. A well-constructed rumor holds our attention. A juicy piece of gossip gives us a naughty thrill. Like the sophisticated version of the "what if" game, they are both a waste of time.

Life is filled with "what if" game players. They come in all shapes and sizes. Some are rank amateurs, but many are serious players of the game. The worst are incorrigible and have achieved near mastery. I call these people spirit takers. They are the ones who whine and complain and bitch and moan until every ounce of spirit, every molecule of energy, is drained from your body. They can extinguish your motivation faster than a pail of water on a candle flame.

You know who spirit takers are because their pockets bulge with kryptonite.

Here's you, walking into the office and feeling upbeat and positive about a recent accomplishment. You've just saved an account from the teeth of death. You worked a voodoo spell on the contract committee so that, despite all the justification to the contrary, the client is going to re-sign for six additional months. You feel great! You are Superman: invincible to mortal laws of mere men. No one could have done what you just did. You're irreplaceable. You've got the goods. A statue should be commissioned in your honor. And, speaking of commission, retaining the client won't hurt the old pocketbook none, that's for sure.

Down the hall comes Peggy, a master "what if" game player and black belt spirit taker.

"How did your presentation go?" she asks.

"Fabulous," you say. "I thought the client was out the door, but in the end, the committee decided to retain us."

"Wow, congratulations," Peggy says, rolling her eyes and feigning halfhearted praise. "How did you overcome our product's horrible performance?"

"I avoided the whole issue of past performance," you say, maybe a bit too smugly. "I told them we'd do better in the future."

"And they believed you?'" Peggy asks, shocked now, opening her eyes like saucers. "Is that client ever gullible! Well, I guess if we buy our competitors' products and rebrand them as ours, we'd have a chance."

Peggy is reaching in her pockets now. What is she digging after? A small voice in the back of your head screams, *"Watch her hands; for God's sake, watch her hands!"*

"I always said that we should have reorganized the technology department years ago." One hand comes out of her pocket, and she nonchalantly flicks a spitball-sized slug of goop on your face. *PLOP.* Then another. *PLOP.* Then in rapid succession two more. *PLOP-PLOP.* "If only we'd have moved our product development shop under Sue last year, then we'd have really seen some improvements. And cost controls? I've got to show you last month's 'Hot Sheet' report. Those bozos in accounting can't balance the general ledger to save their lives; we should have cleaned house a long time ago."

What's in her other hand? Looks like a green snowball. It smells like—yes, I think it is—KRYPTONITE! Is she going to throw it at me? Must dodge it! But, what the—? No feeling in my feet. Legs encased as in Jell-O. Can't bend knees.

"What if we could just erase last year's performance?" Peggy continues, assuming the stance of a baseball pitcher on the mound. "Wouldn't that be great? Think of the client satisfaction we would have if we just did away with everything that's happened since Morris's 'brilliant' Florida merger."

Losing energy units. Must. Fight. Back.

"Let's hope that Morris can turn things around, then," you bravely say. "That would be great."

"Are you kidding? I hear that he might lose his job because of it. His staff is in mass exodus. They say he won't make it to year-end. Good riddance, if you ask me. What if we didn't have to drag his sorry performance around anymore? That's about the only way we'll retain clients."

The windup and the delivery. Splat! A gooey green orb of kryptonite hits you square in the chest. *STEE-RIKE!* And, guess what? Kryptonite sticks! *Who would have thought?* It's as sticky as molasses, impossible to shake off.

"But, I've got to go," Peggy says. "Mel is waiting for this report. Nice seeing you. Congrats on the client news."

No more Superman. Defeated. Overcome by a "what if" player of the first magnitude. There goes Peggy down the hall. She is absolutely oblivious—and lethal. Where's your spirit now? Where did the energy go? It simply dissipated into thin air. Peggy scattered it to the winds.

There you are, walking into a staff meeting. Poor you. "Give us an update," your staff urges. "How did your client meeting go?"

"I don't think we can retain this client much more than six months," you say, a beaten leader.

Because READY Thinkers define reality by avoiding the unnecessary waste and distraction of playing "what if" games and because they walk around with positive outlooks and can-do attitudes, they make tempting targets for spirit takers.

READY Thinkers refuse to make stuff up or to burden reality with the unreal. They have clarity and therefore move with crispness. They have a powerful focus on reality.

Santayana (the philosopher, not Santana the rock and roller) summed it up very succinctly: "One real world is enough."

Most folks go through life carrying the burden of multiple realities. They vigorously create or reaggravate one "what if" scenario after another. This seriously complicates life.

READY Thinking is content with one reality.

chapter 7

The Third Barrier to Reality: Lack of Focus

"The main thing is to keep the main thing the main thing."

This was a very hard chapter to write, given all the distractions.

That's a bummer of a first sentence for a chapter with "Lack of Focus" as its title, but there you go.

My son has a catapult to build for his science project and needs my help to build it—which, of course, means that we will manufacture a catapult that can hurl an egg into outer space. My daughter is asking for help in geography and needs to know what country lies between Nicaragua and El Salvador (it's Honduras). My wife and I have a dinner party to go to this evening, and I am conjuring an excuse to get out of going. Tomorrow is the Easter holiday, with some of our extended family, but not all, joining us for the day's feast. I have to refer to the updated "Baker Family Relationship Matrix" to find out who is getting along with whom during this particular holiday season. Tax time is upon us, and I have to gather my documents. While I'm at it, I should catch up on paying the bills. The mute button is the only thing that works on the TV's remote control for some mysterious reason. New this morning: the laptop gives me pop-up messages warning me that e-mails are no longer secure. I brought home work from the office, but it's sunny with warm temperatures outside; can't say I'll be getting it done.

So goes the voice in my head. My mind is racing, far too fast for me to control. Like a taunting bully, my mind torments me with a steady but seemingly random stream of images, thoughts, ideas, worries, and self-inflicted "what if" games. I debate both sides of mundane issues. I send myself reeling to the past to worry about missed opportunities. I rehearse life as it might happen. I am playing, unsupervised, in my head. I am every-where but in the "now," and it is exhausting.

Where are you? As you read this, what are you thinking?

Perhaps you're not here. I wouldn't be surprised. Hell, I'm checked out too. You've let your mind take charge, and it's gone roaming. It's driving the bus, and you're just a passenger. You're not present. You're somewhere else.

It's not your fault.

After all, you have an addiction.

You're addicted to thinking. You're like a junkie who needs the next fix. Face it: you're compulsive about thinking.

Don't believe it? Try this Two-Minute Drill.

TWO-MINUTE DRILL
OBTAINING ATTENTION

You will need to use some sort of an alarm. Set it for five minutes from now. I know that it says a "Two-Minute Drill." Sorry. *Stop being so anal retentive.* If you don't have access to an alarm, ask someone to call you in five minutes. If you can't arrange for this, establish some signal (the flight attendant making an announcement, the start of the next commercial on the radio, the arrival of someone into your office, whatever) to rouse you from your contemplation.

Quiet yourself as described in Chapter Three. As you quiet yourself, attempt to turn off your thinking mind. As your mind plays its tricks on you—dredging up memories, stimulating worries, randomly generating thoughts—don't judge or become attached to this thinking. Let these thoughts pass and gently return to your contemplation.

When the alarm sounds, document what is on your mind:

_____

_____

_____

_____

You can do this exercise in a variety of ways.

- Next time you are stopped at a traffic light. What were you thinking? Quiet yourself. Use this as a call to reflection.

continues ➤

> When the light turns green and traffic starts to move, notice where your head was.
> - When your child is speaking to you, at the sound of the word "Dad" or "Mom," come to an awareness of what you were thinking. Were you listening?
> - The next time you load the dishwasher, where is your head?

When I speak to the importance of focus, I ask audience members to be prepared to write exactly what they are thinking when I call out "Ready!"

I start into my speech. I build up steam. I flap around the podium like Fidel Castro. I lash the people in the crowd with clever metaphors and batter them with humor. I'm charismatic, my words beautiful and my voice intoxicating. I call out "Ready!" and here is what gets jotted down:

- Remember bread and milk on the way home.
- Ten pounds by the holidays?
- I forgot to call Mary.
- Seal coat the driveway.

I can't really blame them. It is what their brains have been trained to do. Look at our culture. Who cares about now? Everything is about tomorrow. Culturally, we're living in anticipation of the next big thing that will happen in about 45 days. We never seem to simply enjoy the moment we have.

Prepare for a Two-Minute Drill.

TWO-MINUTE DRILL

UNDIVIDED ATTENTION

Simone Weil once said, "Any undivided attention is prayer." This is a powerful concept for you to reflect on as you do this drill.

To complete this drill, I want you to take the following steps. They may require several days to accomplish, or perhaps they can be achieved relatively quickly:

- Identify someone in your life whom you miss, are worried about, have lost touch with, or want to pray for.
- Then, make it a point to physically meet that individual: in person, face to face, one on one. Upon seeing that person, eliminate all distractions from your environment and focus your full attention on him or her.

Don't answer the phone. Don't read a newspaper. Don't rifle through the mail. Don't turn on the television. Don't surf the Web. Don't eat or drink. Avoid catching the eyes of passersby. Don't hold a side conversation. Don't get interrupted. Don't get distracted.

Engage this person with *closeness*. Connect with him or her by asking a question or prompting conversation. Listen. Listen deeply. Make eye contact. Don't listen while simultaneously thinking about the next thing you are going to say. Just listen. When there is a pause, let there be a pause. Don't let the silence interrupt your focus. Be totally in the moment with this person.

You may find that under such intense attention, the person you are with begins to feel uncomfortable. He or she may even get suspicious of your intentions. Calm him or her by gently touching his or

continues ➤

her arm or showing a kind smile. Be reassuring. You can even tell the truth, that you simply want to give your undivided attention.

You will find a calmness come over you. Your time with the other person will become sanctified by your focus. You will feel a powerful connection.

Practice this exercise with your children this evening when you get home from work. You have only a few minutes with them between the time you arrive and the time they go to bed. During this time, give them the full measure of your attention. Treat it as sacred time. Let nothing interrupt your focus. No e-mailing, balancing checkbooks, or scanning the mail or TV news. Just you and them.

Practice this exercise with your spouse or significant other. Attempt to connect in this way at least once a day. Sit and simply talk to each other. Tune everything else out, especially the kids.

If you do this, you will discover a period of your day that gives you great reward. You will truly connect with another human being. You'll bond with your children. You will establish a standard of intimacy with your partner.

After a while, you will look forward to these periods with great anticipation, and you will look back on them with great fondness.

Our minds are programmed to be constantly elsewhere. On the TV program *Everybody Loves Raymond*, the character of Debra confronts her husband about his constant apprehension:

Debra: Raymond, just enjoy the moment.
Raymond (shrugging):   I have no training for that.

Prepare for a Two-Minute Drill.

TWO-MINUTE DRILL
900 SECONDS TO FOCUS

Get yourself comfortable. Wherever you are—at home, at work, on a plane, or on a train—get in a position that feels relaxed to you. Take some deep breaths and try to calm yourself. Here's the exercise:

> *Stop thinking. For the next 15 minutes—900 little seconds—turn your mind completely off. Don't think of one thing. Simply reach into your mind and hit the "off" switch. Do it right now. Don't worry; I'll wait right here until you're back.*

Some people may feel that this exercise is silly and a waste of time.

"There's nothing wrong with how much I think," you may be tempted to say. "Thinking is good. It's essential. It got me to where I am today. It leads to accomplishment and achieves order in my world. Without it, I couldn't analyze or discriminate; that's chaos."

The mind is unquestionably a great tool—but it is just a tool. When not needed, it can be turned off. If you can't stop it, isn't that a problem? Like the addict whose drug is stronger than himself or herself, isn't it possible that your drug—the incessant thinking you do every day—is stronger than you? If you can't turn it off for 15 minutes, 15 inconsequential minutes, aren't you out of control? Isn't that chaos?

When you quiet the mind, you can begin to listen. True listening comes without opinion or prejudice. It leads to learning. As Debashis Chatterjee says in his book *Leading Consciously*, "When listening is very deep, the listener is in touch with the spirit behind the speaker's words."

Prepare for a Two-Minute Drill.

Two-Minute Drill

Multitasking and Communication

Some people believe that multitasking (spreading your attention around to many tasks at the same time) increases productivity. I'll leave them to that delusion. Multitasking suboptimizes multiple efforts and multiple outcomes. My faith is in the person with one iron in the fire.

I do know this for a fact:

You cannot communicate effectively while multitasking.

There really isn't anything to contemplate. This is truth.

Some people don't believe that it is possible to stop thinking—even for a moment. But that's not true. All of the great religious and spiritual traditions have a clear representation of the "inner peace" and silence that comes with prayer and meditation. Mystics walk around all day not thinking, yet they are fully conscious and extremely aware. They are fully engaged in the present moment. They appear detached but exist in a high state of attention. They neither judge the present through the lens of the past nor use the present as simply a staging area for something that might happen in the future. In Eastern philosophies, this state of mind is sometimes described as being of no mind: a gap in thought that leads to peace and calmness and allows great awareness and great alertness.

Many folks will find this to be a bunch of bull. "Measure it!" they'll scream. "Looking at one's belly button never moved the production line faster or shipped more product. This type of gobbledygook is what detracts from throughput and productivity. The essence of commerce is to outhustle, outwork, and, yes, outthink the competition. The idea of bringing 'no mind' to the concept of business leadership is akin to planting a garden without using seeds."

Ever see a Zen garden?

We're used to seeing gardens exploding with color and beauty, varieties of flowers cascading everywhere. Or we're used to tending to vegetable gardens, vibrant with plants and produce.

To our Western sensibilities, Zen gardens seem stark, austere, and vaguely intimidating: a wooden-edged box with raked sand, a few rocks scattered randomly throughout. Going from a flower garden to the Zen garden couldn't be more disorienting.

Zen gardens go back 5,000 years and come in many shapes and sizes, but they all have one thing in common: they seek to do away with more. Their value lies not in providing stimulation for our senses but in encouraging contemplation by giving a time-out for our senses. Zen gardens allow those with a presence of mind—and the desire—to experience enlightenment firsthand.

The vast potential that simplicity and stillness hold is reflected in the words of poet William Blake:

> To see a world in a grain of sand,
> And a heaven in a wild flower,
> Hold infinity in the palm of your hand
> And eternity in an hour.

Our thinking mind is much like the garden analogy. Our bias is to fill all unused space and not permit a moment's idleness. Our heritage is one of hardworking people who taught us that more is better, that a competitive edge comes from physical vigor and intellectual stamina. Our ancestors lorded over the land. They bent it to their will.

Today, we crow about our crammed calendars. All of our appointments are urgent. We multitask. We plow through our overscheduled days and leave sound and fury in our wake. We press for more productivity and sweat efficiency out of every pore. We fill idle moments with thought.

Thinking, though, is not synonymous with focus. Focus requires us to think less and be aware more. Unfocused people deliver poor execution.

In a *Time* magazine essay, Major General Robert Scales (Ret.) wrote about the first sergeant he served with in Vietnam. Scales ultimately served for 34 years in the Army, but in Vietnam, he was new to war. His first sergeant gave him a piece of advice: "In combat, the main thing is to keep the main thing the main thing. Otherwise you die."

The main thing is to keep the main thing the main thing.

If you want to succeed in life, once in a while you have got to clear out the cerebral clutter. Trying to stay focused by cramming more facts, more emotions, more detail into your skull is like holding a garage sale intending to end up with more junk than when you started. Granted, unlike those in combat, the consequence of you losing focus typically isn't the loss of human life. Still, the costs can be disastrous to living as prosperously and as wholly as possible.

Some people constantly seem to be in crisis: money crisis, relationship crisis, professional crisis. They tell you of all the disasters that have befallen them, the awfulness that surely awaits around the next bend, recent breakdowns and betrayals. These folks never seem to be living a life where things are going well.

After countless fruitless interventions ("I implore you—tell me how I can help!"), one can conclude only that these folks don't want any help. They gain focus by being in crisis. It's how they operate: misfortune as a modus operandi. It's a 24/7 "state of emergency" without which they can't get anything done.

Is that how you want to live? So self-absorbed and self-destructive? To gain focus in your life but at the cost of personal sanity?

Cathy was an individual who worked for me for several years. She was a conversion officer in our new accounts department, the area chartered with accepting new business into our company. Converting new accounts into our business required both outstanding technical skills and solid project management capabilities. Conversion officers were the cream of the crop. Cathy was the consummate professional, always leading with a firm and confident hand. Over the years, she had won much recognition and received many performance awards. She was well compensated and expressed great appreciation for the job she had.

The problem? Every conversion, like clockwork, Cathy would have a major emotional breakdown. She would express complete hopelessness, hyperventilate, and stomp around the office while threatening to quit her job.

Now remember that over the years, Cathy had a perfect track record of hitting her project dates. No one had conducted more conversions in my shop than Cathy. Clients gushed with praise.

Yet . . .

"This client is completely unreasonable," Cathy would shout with clenched fists. "We're never going to get this conversion completed. We'll lose the business. This will never work."

The first time I observed this, I was shocked and panic stricken. I pulled Cathy into my office to see whether I could do anything to help lower her stress level. I offered to get her more resources and urged her to off-load certain tasks to others. I shared with her our company's employee outreach program designed to assist employees going through personal crisis. I called her clients to check in and make sure that everything from their point of view was okay.

And from the clients' point of view, invariably, everything was okay. I weathered the first circumstance and then gritted my teeth and got through the second. By the third, I was a broken man.

"Cathy," I beseeched, "this cannot go on. I cannot deal with you crying in my office anymore. I'm male. I cannot manage this way. What is it about

69

this process that makes you go off the deep end? During every conversion, you stress out about missing deadlines and losing business, but you never do. It always works out."

"Not this time, John," she would say. "Oh, this time, it's different."

This went on for months. I asked Cathy whether she thought a job change might be wise, given the stress she went through during every conversion. She responded with indignation.

"Don't you know what this job means to me?" she'd scream.

I began to realize that these meltdowns coincided with the time in the conversion process that Cathy was least in control. At this point of the process, she had to rely on people other than herself—the client, systems programmers, attorneys, consultants, external vendors, suppliers, prior service providers—to meet crucial deadlines and deliver on key obligations. It was the point in the process where Cathy had the least to do. The heavy lifting for her was done. She was done "doing," so to speak, and had time to think. And, boy, would she get after it:

- "Where did the process break down?"
- "What did I forget?"
- "What happens if so-and-so doesn't deliver?"
- "Did I drop the ball?"
- "What about those documents? Maybe they're incorrect."

On and on she went. Her concerns, fertilized by an overactive imagination, blossomed into crippling anxiety. Without the focus of a specific task, her thinking overwhelmed her.

I spoke to Cathy about this observation and asked her whether she thought there was some truth to it. She denied seeing any connection.

On one occasion when Cathy snapped, I called her into my office. I gave her a specific assignment I had been thinking about for some time.

"Cathy," I said after asking her to sit down, "I have something I need you to do. I need you to work on an assignment, the importance of which requires you to drop what you are doing and take full control of the matter. I estimate that it should take the rest of the afternoon. I'm concerned about your capacity, given that the conversion you are working on is not going well—as you keep reminding me—but, I'm convinced of its importance and the necessity to make this your number-one priority."

She was all ears.

"Cathy, today is Thursday, and on Thursdays, they hold the farmer's market down on the mall. It looks great outside. The sun is shining, and I hear the weather is absolutely marvelous. It is one of those days that shouldn't be wasted cooped up staring at a computer screen. So here is what I want you to do: I want you to go down to the farmer's market and buy me an apple."

Cathy stopped writing in her notepad. She wasn't sure whether she had heard me right.

"You want me to buy you an apple?" she asked.

"Affirmative," I said. "Before you ask any more questions, let me finish the assignment. I don't want just any old apple, Cathy. I want the best apple in the entire market. I want you to find me the most perfect apple. I don't care what variety you select, but it obviously has to be blemish free, no bruises, with the perfect size and the perfect color. I want you to spend some time thinking about how you'll attack this problem. The farmer's market stretches several city blocks, and I have no idea how many vendors sell apples. It's up to you to get the best one."

Cathy set her ears back.

"This is insulting," she barked through clenched molars. "I am a professional, John, and my job description doesn't have anything in it about going down to the mall and buying you fruit. You have some gall in asking me to do something like this."

I let that hang in the air for a moment.

"Galling or not, I am asking you to do it. I know you are a professional and you can refuse this request. If you are insulted by it, that is your choice. I wouldn't ask if I didn't think it was important."

Cathy glared at me for what seemed like an hour. Ironically, the color in her face, although I chose not to point this out, matched the crimson red of a perfectly ripe Haralson.

"Fine," she curled her lips and hissed. "I'll get your stupid apple."

I gave her a couple of dollars, and she stormed out of my office.

"Don't forget the change," I shouted to her. Not really, but I thought about it.

Cathy was gone less than seven minutes.

She came bursting into my office at a dead sprint and threw the apple down so hard that it knocked over my desk clock, doing neither much good.

"There's your damn apple. Are you done humiliating me? Everyone thinks you're a nut job for asking me to go buy you an apple, and they think I'm a fool for doing it for you. I hope you're satisfied."

In a quiet voice, I said, "Cathy, please sit down. We need to talk."

She reluctantly took a seat, crossed her arms before her, and leaned back, way back, in her chair.

"You and I have been talking about your behavior over the past several months, how you stress out and visibly break down and how difficult I find that behavior to accept. It is disruptive and unprofessional. It affects me as the leader of this department. It affects the team you work with. It impacts your clients. I have wracked my brain to find a way to work through this with you, but you continue to load yourself up with unnecessary anxiety. This has limited your effectiveness and has stopped you from being the type of leader you could be within the organization."

I took a look at the apple she had bought me.

"Today, with the weather like it is, shouldn't be spent indoors. I thought by asking you to focus on a task that required you to go outside—taking your time, walking among the colors and sounds of the various stalls, smelling the wonderful aromas, talking to the farmers—that you would enjoy yourself and stop thinking about all the imaginary things going wrong at work. The apple assignment wasn't intended to humiliate you. It was an effort to get you to focus on something enjoyable.

"During the seven minutes you were gone, after you stormed out of my office, you inexplicably ignored the sights and sounds and smells of the farmer's market. You didn't feel the sun on your skin. You didn't notice the warm temperatures. Was there a breeze? The people you passed, how many were there? Did they smile at you? You missed them all. You were so obsessed with the emotion surrounding the apple that you missed the world."

I knew Cathy was still livid because I could count her pulse rate on her throbbing aorta.

"Similar to your work on your conversion projects, you chose to load up the apple assignment with needless stress. Would people think you're stupid for doing it? Was I crazy for asking you? Or was I being mean? Should you feel humiliated? Cathy, I just wanted an apple. A simple request. You turned it into an ordeal."

She stood abruptly and left my office in a huff. I wish I could say that, after thoughtful consideration, she became enlightened and never again lost focus or perspective with her job. Nope, didn't happen. Cathy continued to provide outstanding service to our firm and our clients and—true to form—freaked out during one painful week of every single conversion. I think she hid it better. I think after our talk she became more aware of her impact and adjusted her style to be less overt with her emotions, but she never became aware of how her mind mastered her every move.

Without focus, we are poor leaders and are less effective than we could be.

It is a simple call to action: stop thinking so much.

READY Thinkers think less.

chapter 8

The Fourth Barrier
to Reality: Fear

"Hell possessed their hearts and minds."

Years ago, I found myself on a physical fitness kick that had me working out about five or six times a week. Variety being the spice of life, when the gym's owner asked whether I would be interested in taking up boxing, I soon found myself hitting heavy bags, jumping rope, throwing medicine balls, and shadowboxing in front of mirrors.

A regulation-sized boxing ring was erected in the middle of his gym, and my fellow students and I danced around aiming punches at imaginary opponents. We were told to throw our punches, as Mike Tyson would, "with bad intentions." At the end of each workout, we hit the speed bag to bring tempo and quickness to our hands.

After about a month of this, the owner announced that an old friend of his was making a run to get back into the pro-level boxing business and was interested in sparring a few rounds as a way to shake off the rust.

"I need three volunteers to spar one round each," I remember him saying. "Don't worry. He's been out of the fight game for a few years. You'll wear full headgear, and we won't be going full speed."

I had 30 days of training under my belt, so I, of course, was the first to climb into the ring. I was full of energy. The gloves on my hands felt as light as balloons. After jumping rope and jogging and doing leg presses up the wazoo, my legs felt like two oak trees. The guys in my corner shouted encouragement.

"You got this guy, John!"

"Remember: it's only a sparring match. Don't go full out."

"Save some of him for us!"

A trainer strapped protective gear on my head, shoved a guard over my teeth, and squirted water into my mouth. It was just like every boxing sequence I had ever seen. I was stoked and ready to go.

My opponent lumbered through the gym and groaned as he crawled between the ropes into the ring. His body was as thick and gelatinous as a big hunk of Spam. He was an extremely hairy man. *The PGA cuts its rough shorter!* He also was an extremely tattooed man, a mighty off-putting combination. It was odd not knowing where his body hair ended and the tattoos began. *How does he get a date?* In large Gothic letters scrawled across the top of his chest, he had his name spelled out: MACE.

Just like in the movies, we met in the middle of the ring to get instructions and to tap gloves. Up close, I noticed Mace's flat nose and a scar that bisected his right eyebrow. He smelled awful. He hadn't shaved for days, and he was breathing right in my face, so it was easy to establish the fact that he hadn't brushed his teeth in a while either. I sized him at least 20 pounds overweight: fleshy and soft, as they say in the fight biz. I figured I'd wear him down with my superior cardio training. Plus, Mace stood almost a foot shorter than me, another advantage.

The trainer wiped down my face with an old towel. I was surprised at how much I was sweating. Hot headgear, hot lights, hot blood. *Let's go!* The bell rang, and the first round was on.

Mace marched over to me and clocked me three times in the nose. He hit only with his jab, but it had—as they say in the fight business—a lot on it. In fact, it beheld great power. It spoketh to me and said unto me, "Behold, thou shalt call me 'Mr. Mace.' Seek no more, sayeth I, for verily on this day, know that I am your daddy."

Many thoughts raced through my brain. The first was the most disheartening. "Did he just hit me once, or did he hit me three times?" A bad thought. Unsettling. Worrisome in the vein of "I know not this thing they call boxing." Funny how a fellow standing in a boxing ring ends up surprised to be looking at the business end of a leather mitt. *This was unexpected?* A nettlesome thought. One to ponder but for the fact it was quickly supplanted by a second thought—no, more like a deep, instinctual, primitive longing—not to ever be hit again.

Next to flash through my mind, go figure, was how strange the glove smelled. It had a scent with which I was not familiar and therefore could not quite place. Ah, quickly it dawned upon me. They don't launder boxing gloves.

Ever.

The accumulated snot, spit, sweat, and blood from innumerable oozing noses and spewing mouths and discharging armpits amassed through countless rounds sparred by the most impure and hairy of men, fermented to the finest of bouquets in dank, spore-producing lockers and then thrown casually into the gumbo of old yellowed jock straps and unwashed and soiled athletic socks, had just penetrated very far into my nose, had instantly breached the mucus membrane, and was now overwhelming all components of my autoimmune system. *I am going to catch something very bad.*

Of course, I felt many things, immediately and simultaneously. First was pain. Because Spam boy was a half-foot shorter, his jab was at an upward angle that fully appreciated my complete nasal septum. He didn't hit my nose as much as he jacked it up and in, overcrowding bone, cartilage, and tissue into what's an already relatively tight cavity. An unnatural act, defying the physical body's divine order. A freak combination of anatomy and physics. Who would've thought?

I also felt anger, not at Mr. Mace, interestingly enough, but at the makers of the protective headgear. As peculiar as it sounds, the parts of my head being protected weren't the parts Mr. Mace was aiming for. My nose was a perfect target, an exposed and inspirational beacon. Next time I'd be going into the ring wearing a welder's mask—anything but the stupid thing I was wearing, which would have provided great protection if Mr. Mace was interested in giving me a noogie. Three seconds into our match, I had found out he wasn't.

And, most of all, I felt fear.

The mind-numbing, bladder-emptying kind of fear that explodes from the most primal parts of the brain and takes over every single one of your motor neurons and makes bodily fluids head for the exits. The kind of fear that fuses your knee joints so you run stricken around the ring looking like Frankenstein being chased by fire-toting villagers. The kind of fear that turns boxing gloves into medicine balls. The kind of fear that makes you want to cry out for your mommy to help save you from the bad man.

I spent the next two minutes and 57 seconds turning our sparring match into a footrace. It was undignified. Mr. Mace would angle me into a corner (*How did he get so light on his feet all of a sudden?*) and I would escape by any means necessary. I'd hit at him with my open palm—the famous slap defense. I reverted to the windmill style of punching used when I was seven years old. I'd cover up my face, tuck my elbows as close to my kidneys as possible, and try to dash by him. I would grab him—*oh, that lovely, damp, hirsute man*—and hold on for dear life until the referee would call me a girl and wedge us apart.

I avoided taking any more head shots, but despite my defenses (or because of them), Mr. Mace landed body punches pretty much at will. Each time he connected, the pain would announce itself in my loins, circumnavigate my midsection, catch a breather in my lumber region, enter the autobahn of my spinal column, and, like nasty in-laws who don't call in advance, jarringly pull into my lower cranial cortex. The fear would explode again.

The bell came after a year and a half.

I felt like I had hauled rock up a hill for an entire summer. My arms were sore and my legs exhausted. My nose whistled like a songbird. I was hyperventilating, with my mouth as open as a garage door, but I still couldn't seem to get any oxygen in my lungs. My skin was chafed red with interesting patterns of welts where Mace's grubby beard had scored into it like a cheese grater. My arms were already yellowing with advanced notice of bruising. The lights over the ring felt like a sun bed.

I returned to the corner to see that my comrades had turned completely white. So brazen minutes before, they couldn't get enough spit in their mouths to even whimper a charitable "Good job" or "You hung in there." They had it worse than I did: they saw their future and knew what was coming.

I look back at that episode—the last time I got in the boxing ring, by the way—and realize how foolish my training had been, how unprepared I was for the ring. It wasn't that I was out of shape; I was in the best shape of my life. It wasn't that I didn't know how to move around the ring or how to punch.

It was because I didn't know what it was like to *get* hit. To *take* a punch. To get hurt. To feel fear course through my veins and to deal with it. To overcome it and move on.

Looking back, it's almost naive to think I could have felt ready for a boxing match without ever having gotten into the ring with someone intent on hitting back. Often, this is the case with life as well: we naively expect to live pain free, and so we are unprepared when it arrives.

A "Mr. Mace" populates every part of our lives.

Maybe it's the irate driver with road rage.

Or the hothead who says you cut in line at the coffee shop.

Or the friend with the hair-trigger temper.

Or the coworker who rudely interrupts you when you are addressing a group on a topic of key importance.

Or the coach who berates you in front of others.

The overdemanding boss. The boorish colleague. The unethical competitor. The unreasonable client. Fear can strike at school, on the freeway, at church, in the boardroom, during a sales pitch, at a staff meeting. Wherever people tend to display a need to dominate, fear will inevitably play a role.

Fear comes, by its nature, when you are not looking. You cannot organize it into your day. It lurks, waiting for your defenses to be down and for a moment of weakness to appear.

You can succumb to fear or attack it head-on. Succumbing is no way to live. We take on the victim's facade and perpetuate a lot in life as losers to the world's bullying.

Attacking it head-on turns us into the very people we don't want to be: hyperaggressive, easily offended, and quick to lash out. We move through our daily lives like we're living a video game and expecting attacks to come from every angle, striking out at each and every threat, real or perceived, and leaving carnage in our wake.

There is a third choice: to welcome conflict and appreciate the fear, to learn how to use fear instead of having it use us.

Aikido, for example, is a dancelike martial art that emphasizes redirection of aggression over direct confrontation. Unlike other martial arts, such as karate, aikido uses no blocking techniques. A student of aikido, an *aikidoka*, learns the art of blending with an incoming attack. He or she is taught how to effectively "give way" rather than risk a direct clash with a stronger opponent. The *aikidoka* is taught to stay calm in the face of danger, master his or her fear, be exceedingly aware of the surroundings, and attain a superior position of defense. The goal of an aikido practitioner is to end an attack without unnecessarily injuring the assailant. A master of this martial art simply moves from the aggressor's line of attack without striking a single blow, oftentimes sending the aggressor sprawling to the ground.

Change exposes people to risk. With risk comes the chance of failure. That's where the fear comes in and most people pull back. They envision dire consequences, nearly always overly dramatic. They step back and become paralyzed. They duck in anticipation of imagined blows to come; they pride themselves on keeping their heads low. They lock themselves into the safety net of conformity and enslave themselves into mediocrity.

READY Thinking is learning to become someone able to deal with the fear that comes with change and uncertainty, to move through uncharted territory by using fear to an advantage.

That takes experience. No matter what yardstick you want to measure yourself with, it is inevitable that you need to take on new things—strange and difficult things—in order to grow. The world is filled with competitors who want to kick butt: your butt. They'd love it if you would make an easier target by standing still. Staying the "same" is not possible. The opposite of growth isn't the status quo; it's death. Growth is a requirement, whether it be for a healthy life, a healthy relationship, or a healthy company. To grow requires risk taking. Risk means possible failure. The idea of failing is scary. To be able to use your fear is a hallmark of READY Thinking.

There is no cute formula to achieve this; you have to be willing to take your lumps. The call to master your fear is as old as our time on earth. It is a quest that humans have been on since creation.

Centuries ago, illiterate tribes of nomads wandered Europe in search of food, work, and shelter. For safety, they used to stop at large fire pits, communal gathering spots, to rest and gain warmth and be protected by the flames.

Around these fire pits spoke storytellers. One story—a myth, really—was that of Beowulf. You remember the story of Beowulf, told for more than a thousand years; unfathomably written in old English by some anonymous scribe; a book your English teacher made you read back in the tenth grade, which you didn't because it was impenetrable and, unlike the movie, there was no Angelina Jolie in the book.

Beowulf Was a READY Thinker

Like most kingdoms, that of Hrothgar was filled with warriors who both celebrated excessively in the great hall and sought glory in bloody battlefields. Hrothgar was a patriarchal king, wise and caring, and his reign was one of prosperity. That is, until one night after the day's feasting had ended, and the tall tales had been spoken, and the last of the wine had been drunk. As the candlelight dimmed and the kingdom slept, there came out from the primordial swamp a monster not before seen in the realm. Enraged by the scene of sated and sleeping warriors, the evil beast devoured 30 of the kingdom's most honored knights.

This, one could guess, came as quite a wake-up call to the citizenship. They called this monster Grendal, and while the king vowed for revenge, they soon discovered that Grendal was something of a glutton and his appetite wasn't satisfied with a mere 30 warriors. Night after night, for 12 long years, despite the ambushes they laid for him, Grendal invaded the kingdom and laid waste to more good men.

> *"Again and again the enemy of man*
> *Stalking unseen, struck terrible*
> *and bitter blows . . .*
> *The council lords sat there*
> *daily to devise some plan*
> *What might be best for brave-hearted Danes to*
> *control these terror-raids . . .*

Hell possessed their hearts and minds . . .
Woe to him who must in
terrible trial entrust his soul
To the embrace of the burning, banished from
thought of change or comfort."

Hrothgar realized he was no longer the ruler of his kingdom; Grendal was. In desperation, he sent for Beowulf, both calling on the brave warrior to slay the evil Grendal and initiating what could have been the world's first consulting gig. Beowulf arrived with his team, cleverly set a trap for Grendal, and heroically slew the monster. The kingdom rejoiced and laughed in triumph over Grendal's death. The grandest party of them all was called for; a magnificent banquet was spread, and feasting and drinking commenced. Upon Beowulf was bestowed a mountain of glory and gold. All was well once again in the kingdom of Hrothgar.

That is, until Grendal's mother came crawling out of the swamp. Perhaps not surprisingly, she was royally pissed off. The kingdom was once again set upon by a terrible—and this time vengeful—beast.

Beowulf, the slayer of monsters, had a problem. Hero one minute, chump the next. The kingdom called for action—and he'd better make it quick: *"We hired you to solve our beast problem, and here we are still having this conversation."* Beowulf intended to ambush Grendal's mother but to no avail. She was cleverer than her son, and despite his best plans, he could not trap her into battle on land.

continues ➤

83

This is where the story turns interesting. Imagine Beowulf standing at the edge of the primeval swamp, a place so vile nothing grows around it but stunted bushes and grotesque trees, leafless and sooty. Scattered on the shore are the skulls and bones of the monster's earlier meals. The air is filled with the acrid scent of sulfur. The turbid reddish-brown water boils and steams, not only from some supernatural heat but also from wicked and nameless creatures slithering just beneath the surface. The air is stagnant and polluted.

Beowulf has come here to the swamp's edge because he has arrived at a most unpleasant conclusion. To kill Grendal's mother, he cannot wait in Hrothgar's golden hall. No, he must get into the dark, slimy water of the monster's domain, swim down to her cave, and do battle with her in her own lair. And, he must do it alone.

Swimming down to the monster's cave takes him most of the day, and when he arrives, he discovers that the weapon he has taken with him, the legendary sword named Hrunting, which has never failed in battle or seen defeat, is of no use to him in the monster's lair. (*Can't you see him smacking his forehead?*) The sword's edge, razor sharp as it is, cannot cut through the thick, heinous skin of the beast. In the ferocious battle with Grendal's mother, Beowulf grasps an enormous sword, one from a giant who must have done battle with her in times long past, and with a heroic thrust, he cuts off the monster's head.

This is an age-old parable about fear: fear that comes—when else?—in the middle of the night, fear that crawls out of some dark and unsettled place in our psyche and rules our kingdom, fear that unexpectedly interrupts our celebrations and peace of mind, fear that lives down there in the swamp—our swamp.

Like Beowulf, we cannot talk fear away. We cannot lay in ambush for it during the light of day. Most fear isn't rational, and so it cannot be attacked with traditional and familiar weapons such as logic or reason. We have to summon the courage to get into the swamp and face fear where it lives.

Prepare for a Two-Minute Drill.

Two-Minute Drill

Masks of Fear

Fear doesn't always come in packages as easy to recognize as Mr. Mace or Grendal or his mother. Fear wears a number of disguises. At the nucleus of certain emotions is fear. *I fear I won't get my fair share in life, so I feel selfish. I fear that I cannot be happy unless I am with another person, so I feel lonely. I procrastinate because I fear I will not succeed.* What do you fear when you feel:

Envy?_____

Resentment?_____

Procrastination?_____

Controlling?_____

Betrayed?_____

Lonely?_____

Detached?_____

continues ➤

Hopeless? _____

Greedy? _____

Selfish? _____

Egotistic? _____

Unworthy? _____

Judgmental? _____

You cannot fight a foe you do not recognize. Consider how you will recognize fear in your life, in all its masks.

Once you have distinguished the fear, embrace it. Greet it. Become familiar with how your mind and body react to it. Recognize its affect on you and your life. See how it reacts to truth. See whether it holds its shape.

For example, if you feel envious, ask yourself why you fear someone else's success or good fortune. "I fear I won't achieve that level of success," you might say. Or, "I haven't seen good fortune in my life, and I fear I won't."

Go further with this exercise. Confront the fear. "I understand this is fear. It isn't rational. It narrows my mind and clouds my thinking. I notice my heart beating more rapidly and see that my face is getting red. This is how I react to fear. In the face of this fear, I remind myself that, even if success and good fortune aren't right around the corner, I can be happy just as I am today. Someone else's lot in life, good or bad, has no true bearing on my choice to be happy."

Now bring the light. Rather than let the fear clutter your mind, focus on a constructive behavior. You might choose to read a chapter in an inspiring book or listen to upbeat music. You might spend time on a hobby you've been neglecting or begin a project you've been putting off. You might discuss your concerns with a mentor or trusted therapist.

You will do these constructive things in the presence of fear, but your fear will be revalued. It might still be in attendance, but you have weakened its hold over you. Time and patience are your two best allies. By repeatedly working through this process, you will find a means to recognize your fear as it arises, face it, and, far from losing your bearings, have the facility to use it to your advantage.

Prepare for a Two-Minute Drill.

TWO-MINUTE DRILL

FEAR OF FAILURE

Consider the fear of failure: a common, if not ubiquitous, fear of the ambitious.

Then consider the following quote by Hokusai Katsushika, one of Japan's premier artists, who some say literally created Japanese landscape art. He wrote this mini-autobiography at the age of 83:

> *"From the age of six, I could draw forms and objects. By 50 I had turned out an infinite number of drawings. But I am not happy about anything I did before 70. Only at 73 did I begin to understand the true form*

continues ➤

and nature of birds, fish and plants. By 80 I had made a lot of progress. At 90 I will begin to get to the root of it all. By 100 I will have reached a Superior State in art, undefinable, and by 110, every dot and line will be living. I challenge those who live as long as me to see if I keep my word."

How does this quote make you feel about your journey through life?

_____

_____

Do you think of yourself still on a mission of discovery, one that has yet to be completed? Why or why not?

_____

_____

How would you feel if at age 70, you were not happy with anything you had done?

_____

_____

What stops you from feeling the same type of swagger that Katsushika feels when he confidently boasts, "At 90 I will begin to get to the root of it all"?

_____

_____

How would you redefine the concept of "failure" if you knew that you would not achieve your goals until you were 100?

_____

_____

You are going to take your lumps in life, and fear will be their companion. In *The Alchemist*, Paulo Coelho writes, "So why is it important to suffer? Because, once we have overcome the defeats—and we always do—we are filled with a greater sense of euphoria and confidence."

Imagine filling your life up with a greater sense of euphoria and confidence.

This must be what true living is all about: confidence, beauty, peace, joy, and growth—on the other side of fear. Be a READY Thinker. Get in the swamp. Take your lumps. Master your fear.

chapter 9

The E in READY
Thinking: Enlarging

"You can always amend a big plan,
but you can never expand a little one."

The most important thing you can ask in READY Thinking is "What's in it for me?"

No, you say, *I don't think so!*

Don't fool yourself, kid. We're all in it for something. Life has only three major motivations.

One, I do what I do because it makes me feel good.

Two, I do what I do because if I didn't, I would feel worse.

Or, three, I'm a saint.

As the great Sufi would say: "A saint is one until he or she knows it." Wrap your head around that for a while.

While most of us like what we do, the reason we work is to provide for ourselves and our families. We're in it for the same thing. People aren't all that different when it comes right down to it. While we take different paths, we all have the same basic motivation: "What's in it for me?"

A high-flying executive once expressed his exasperation that when he arrived to work on Sunday, no one else was in the office. "How can people tell me they're so busy," he'd complain, "when it's a ghost town in here on the weekends?"

The response to him: "What are you avoiding at home on Sundays?"

There was something in it for him to work on Sundays. While most people chose to take this day off from work, this man chose not to. That might have made him a martyr, but it didn't make him a saint.

READY Thinking recognizes that "What's in it for me?" is on the tips of our lips: our spouse's, our friends', our employees', our clients', our prospects'.

A healthy marriage is one where partners pay attention to the needs and wants of each other, essentially asking, "What's in it for this person to be married to me?" Friends ask, "What's in it for me to be a friend to this person?" Clients ask, "What's in it for me to do business with this person?"

Prepare for a Two-Minute Drill.

Two-Minute Drill
"What's In It For Me?"

I've got news for you, news that surprises a lot of folks. Just because you haven't heard someone ask you *What's in it for me?* doesn't mean he or she isn't asking the question. That's not necessarily good news.

People don't always express their confusion, unease, or misgivings overtly, but that doesn't mean they aren't there. You have to expressly tell important people in your life what's in it for them. Otherwise, doubt and discomfort inevitably overtake their self-talk.

What's in it for your spouse to be married to you?
What's in it for you?

What's in it for your children to respect you as a parent?
What's in it for you?

What's in it for your employees to work for you?
What's in it for you?

What's in it for your clients to do business with you?
What's in it for you?

What's in it for those you lead to follow you?
What's in it for you?

Employees who work for you hear what's in it for them in two ways.

1. They hear it from their leader.
2. They hear it from competitors.

Sure, it's about the money. It's always about the money. But, it's not *only* about the money.

People want to feel part of something bigger: a robust partnership, a winning team, an energetic business. They want to be part of something that's healthy and growing: an organization that can help them accomplish things that are bigger than the things they can accomplish by themselves. They want their work to be important and to make a difference. Once in a while, we have to re-recruit people by reminding them that what they do is far more important than their daily planner might lead them to believe.

If you aren't talking about an enlarged message, who will? The competition is after the best of what you have. If you haven't communicated an enlarged message to your clients—what your company stands for today and in the years to come—be assured that your competition has.

Prepare for a Two-Minute Drill.

TWO-MINUTE DRILL
SELF TALK

The most important thing you can ask yourself is "What's in it for me?" If you aren't sure how you would answer this question, then the hurricanes of self-doubt and second thoughts will howl. Does this sound like being ready?

What's in it for you to be a leader?

What's in it for you to service your clients?

What's in it for you to go through change?

What's in it for you to be an employee at your company?

You may not overtly acknowledge your qualms (about work, love, friendship, etc.), but they exist. What's your self-talk? Leaders tell people what's in it for them because they want to enlarge the discussion. What are you telling yourself?

In the Bible, Isaiah 54:2, it says, "Enlarge the place of your tent. Let the curtains of your habitation be stretched out. Spare not. Lengthen your cords and strengthen your stakes, for soon you will be bursting at the seams."

I don't know about you, but I want to live "bursting at the seams." I want to live a life that has a "big tent" mentality, where opportunities abound. Harry Truman once said, "You can always amend a big plan, but you can never expand a little one."

Prepare for a Two-Minute Drill.

TWO-MINUTE DRILL

EXPANDING A SMALL PLAN

For the next two minutes, write a few things (e.g., rewards, attributes, characteristics, etc.) that you consider good about where you work. Go!

Prepare for another Two-Minute Drill.

TWO-MINUTE DRILL

AMENDING A LARGE PLAN

For the next two minutes, write **30** things (e.g., rewards, attributes, characteristics, etc.) that you consider good about where you work. Go!

1. _____   11. _____   21. _____

2. _____   12. _____   22. _____

continues ▶

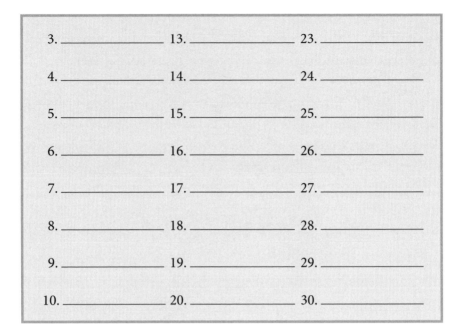

These two drills illustrate the power of an enlarged message. In the first drill, you had a small task; in the second, you were given a larger obligation. Which produced the most attributes? You might not have come up with 30 positive characteristics in two minutes, but you certainly came up with many more than you did in the first drill. By asking you to think of 30 attributes, the drill increased your expectations. It drove more results.

Nothing is more defeating to an organization than when groups of people rally around things that are limiting. Organizations determined to improve client service get hamstrung when everyone around the water cooler is asking about the size of his or her office cube. Sales strategies get stymied when salespeople get stuck on mundane corporate policies. What is disdained within an organization gains power. Marriages get derailed when common resentments are left unattended. Friendships break apart over petty disagreements.

That's why READY Thinking connects leadership to an enlarged message.

In the 1960s, President John Kennedy called upon the country to launch a man into space and land him on the moon. Then to really complicate things, he called for the need to return him safely to Earth.

Wow. That was something—not uncontroversial by the way—that really ignited a generation still somewhat back on its heels due to the Soviet Union's surprise launch of Sputnik. It was a broad, bold message of "can do," beyond the scope of any one person, cosmically risky but vastly invigorating.

Standing before the Berlin Wall, a symbol of communist oppression for more than 25 years, President Ronald Reagan challenged the general secretary of the Soviet Union by demanding, "Mr. Gorbachev, tear down this wall."

Few thought the destruction of the wall was a realistic prospect. The Soviet press agency called the speech "war mongering." Yet, two years later, the wall was destroyed by freedom-loving, sledgehammer-wielding Germans.

You have heard (and maybe delivered) far more diminishing messages:

"Just do it."

"You're lucky you have a job."

"I don't know why we're spending money on that project."

"I don't make the decisions."

We have all worked for a boss or a company that has held the opinion that what's in it for you is "the fact you're getting a paycheck." How demoralizing!

A mentor of mine once told me that in life there are stonecutters and cathedral builders. Which do you want to be?

Some say that leaders must provide hope. But, hope can be naive or manipulative. It can be desperate or exultant, too disconnected from reality. The importance of providing an enlarged message does not negate the need to tie it to reality.

Prepare for a Two-Minute Drill.

Two-Minute Drill
Personal Action Plan

"Enlarging" is an essential part of READY Thinking because in a vacuum, the opposite takes hold: shrinkage (*yikes*), decline, and contraction.

Companies often have mission statements to help shape the dialogue that they want to engage in with their employees and clients. Write your own personal mission statement to help shape your internal dialogue.

The tasks I do during the day are _____.

I do these tasks using _____.

I do these tasks with _____.

I do these tasks because they allow my company to _____

_____.

If these tasks didn't get done, our clients would not _____

_____.

Now, circle the key words in each line and write them below:

_____

_____

My Personal Mission Statement: _____

_____

_____

Here is an example:

The tasks I do during the day are: *I respond to 40 phone calls per day, in order to answer questions and concerns from consumers regarding their financial situations.*

I do these tasks using: *the best technology available, online scripts to ensure accuracy, and other tools to increase my servicing effectiveness.*

I do these tasks with: *a team of six other professionals, each with his or her own unique specialization, demonstrating competence and assuring the clients that they are getting the best answers possible to achieve their financial goals.*

I do these tasks because they allow my company to: *deliver on its larger mission of providing solutions that consumers can rely on.*

If these tasks didn't get done: *our clients would not feel comfortable with their financial situations, they would not have the information they need to make good decisions regarding their financial goals, they would lose trust in my company, and they would seek out solutions at other companies.*

continues ➤

> My Personal Mission Statement: *I give clients comfort and confidence and help them achieve their financial goals by effectively responding to their questions and concerns. In doing so, I and my team generate the confidence and loyalty necessary for our company to maintain a long-term, trust-based client relationship.*

READY Thinkers enlarge their own missions. It starts by looking in the mirror. Nothing gets done that your self-talk doesn't allow. You put up your own barriers within your work and your life. We cannot motivate others to achieve bigger things if we cannot motivate ourselves. I am hard-pressed to think of anything worthwhile accomplished with a defeatist attitude. Can you imagine winning a new sale by saying "I'm likely to fail, so I shouldn't even bother"? Or getting that promotion by saying "I'm completely unqualified and don't deserve the job"?

You may not accomplish everything you envision, but you will never accomplish those things you cannot envision.

I am attracted to people who think highly of themselves, the people who ask "What's in it for me?" not as self-centered egotists but with the idea that something good is in store for them. They attract energy. They get knocked back, sure, but they have faith that circumstances will turn their way. The energy that they greet others with is rejuvenating. They are powerful and charismatic forces within the world.

STAN IS A READY THINKER

On a trip to see one of his largest and most influential clients, Stan arranged to meet at a wonderful restaurant for dinner. The dinner conversation was a gratifying mix of positive feedback about the products and services Stan's company was providing and strong indications that future business would likely be coming his way. The client laced his comments with asides on how wonderful he thought Stan was and how irreplaceable his services were to the future of the account.

Stan should have been beaming, but instead he cleared his throat and began to speak.

"Well, I'm pleased you're happy with our services," Stan said, "but I don't know how long I will be on this account. I've done about as much with you as I think you'll let me. If we are to continue working together, some things will have to change."

The client sat back in his chair and gave Stan a hard look. "What are you suggesting?" he asked.

"You offer your employees so much value," Stan appealed, "but you aren't willing to use all the tools we have available to really make our services stand out and maximize their impact. We can do so much more together—but only if you are willing."

Stan went on to describe a new level of commitment that he was looking for. Not just lip service but renewed dedication to offer programs and services that could profoundly make a difference in the lives of the client's employees. The result, Stan assured him, was a level of performance that he would feel proud to take to his CEO. One he would be pleased to see represented in the trade press. One that could be packaged to influence future legislative outcomes. One that he could hold his head high about, every day, at work.

Whatever it was—the wine, the food, the frank conversation—the night was a roaring success. After years of trying to get

continues ➤

the client to implement key service innovations, the logjam broke, and real momentum ensued.

Later, the client asked Stan what was going through his mind when he brought up his ultimatum at dinner. The client wondered aloud about whether he was bluffing about resigning from the account.

Stan said, "I'm at an age now, and senior enough in the business, to want to do things the right way. If I can, I know I can change lives. If I can't, I'm wasting the time I have left to make a difference in this world."

Stan wasn't bluffing.

Through his self-talk, Stan had enlarged his mission and accomplished a most honorable and far-ranging goal. He could have sat through the dinner, accepting the accolades, but he was determined to do something bolder and make a difference. He believed that he could affect the lives of thousands of people and, through his conviction, convinced a recalcitrant client that he could do the same.

Stan's dinner conversation soon made the rounds throughout his company. Those around him began wondering whether their self-talk had been too limiting. Not every client would sign on to such a bold agenda, they thought, but every client should be given the choice.

READY Thinkers enlarge their mission and the missions of those they influence.

chapter 10

The A in READY Thinking: Accountability

"The buck stops here."

I't's about you.

Either you caused the issue or you have to resolve it.

It's about you.

Modern life has us confused on this issue. We're entertained by reality television reflecting sick relationships or ill-behaved criminals. Scandalous conduct is beamed by satellite from across the globe. We expect and accept obsolescence in the products we buy. We throw around lawsuits—the casino made me gamble all my money, the bartender should have cut me off, the food companies put too much fat in my food—like beads off a Mardi Gras parade. Atrocious service our parents' generation would not have tolerated is so commonplace we no longer bother squawking about it.

We access technology that is architected to insulate human experience. We're comfortable conversing with pleasant-sounding, interactive, prerecorded, digitalized voices. We do business with huge multinational organizations that are as easy to understand as hieroglyphics (but that can save us a buck or two on our next purchase).

We forget the value of accountability.

It's about you.

Either you caused the issue or you have to resolve it.

The "READY Thinking Accountability Matrix" is built around the notion that, no matter the situation, these two factors lead to only four possible outcomes:

1. I caused the issue, **and** I have to resolve it.
2. I caused the issue, **but** someone else has to resolve it.
3. I didn't cause the issue, **but** I have the responsibility to resolve it.
4. I neither caused the issue **nor** have to solve it.

READY Thinking Accountability Matrix

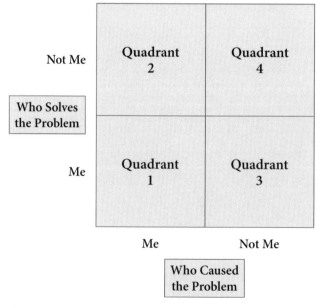

Just as a reminder:

READY Thinking Accountability Matrix

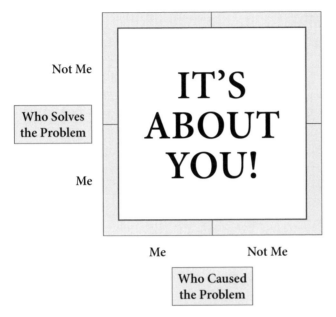

That certainly looks intimidating, doesn't it?

The reason people want to join *your* team is because they believe that the journey *you* lead them on will be worthwhile, the destination *you* take them to will be important, and *your* leadership can get them there. Blow the accountability bond, and don't look back: *your* team will be long gone.

Remember those words we associated with being "READY" in Chapter Three: "forward-looking," "confident," "on your toes," "capable"? None of these words means a thing if you abandon ship at the first sign of bad weather. It's hard to adopt a posture of readiness if your first instinct is to point a finger in reproach.

Taking accountability is not an exercise in fairness, but it doesn't mean being a scapegoat either. READY Thinkers have a willingness to take responsibility for nuanced and complex issues with open minds—but without necessarily changing their minds. Accountability is the practice of practical engagement.

Quadrant 1: Personal Performance

Quadrant 1: You caused the problem, and you are clearly the responsible party for resolving it. This is a common event in both our personal and our professional lives. This quadrant is called "personal performance."

READY Thinking Accountability Matrix

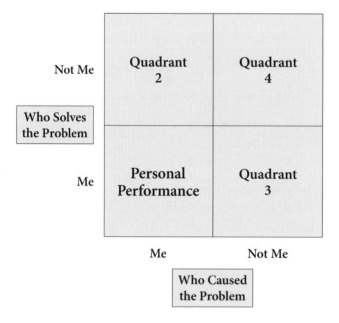

While there is a strong leadership component required in quadrant 1, issues in this box are best handled through the application of management skill. I caused the problem, so I've got to solve it. I thought I could do the task, or complete the job, or fulfill the role, but something went awry, and now I have to clean up the mess.

As managers of our lives, we work to get as much of the unknown into the known and assess our personal readiness to do the job at hand. Have I successfully done it before? Have I had the proper training or education? Do I have all the necessary tools and resources?

Because we're imperfect human beings, quadrant 1 is not entirely avoidable. Complications in our daily lives, plus the basic fact that we are not infallible, plus too many demands and too little time: this formula means that sometimes even when we are completely capable of accomplishing a task, we still might screw it up.

Quadrant 1 is cleaning up after yourself.

KOBE BRYANT IS A Q1 READY THINKER

Blessed with a surplus of athletic talent, Kobe Bryant quickly established himself as one of the premier players in the history of the National Basketball Association. His proficiency is unique in that he is both an elite scorer and an exceptional defensive player. His preparation off the court and his consistent intensity on it serve to elevate the performance of his entire team.

After the 2007 season, Bryant realized that his jump shot percentage had dipped slightly. Upon review of game film, he noticed that due to a nagging finger injury, the rotation on the basketball as it released from his hand differed slightly from shot to shot. During the off-season, Bryant hit the gym and made 1,000 jump shots a day. He didn't shoot 1,000 shots; he *made* 1,000. Every day.

"You don't practice taking shots," Bryant said. "You practice making them."

Prepare for a Two-Minute Drill.

TWO-MINUTE DRILL
PERSONAL PERFORMANCE

It's calendar time. Open your calendar and study the way you have used your time during the past week. The first step of this drill is to identify those blocks of time you have spent (A) correcting issues that you have caused yourself and/or (B) dealing with employees who have made an error and now need to correct the situation themselves. These are Q1 situations.

Notice how much time is being spent in this quadrant. Does it seem reasonable to you? Analyze the data to see whether any trends emerge: certain standards that are habitually being missed, tasks that aren't getting done, or items that appear to fall into error far too frequently. Is there an individual who is requiring abnormally high levels of managerial oversight or leadership support on tasks that he or she should have mastered?

Q1 situations can be limited but not completely prevented. As you look out to the next five days, establish an action plan to limit the amount of time you intend to spend on Q1 behavior.

For those situations in which you yourself erred and now need to take personal accountability to resolve, are you:

- Allocating proper priority to the situation?
- Carving out enough time to accomplish the task?
- Acknowledging any personal gaps in training and/or experience?
- Seeking out the appropriate level of support?

For those situations in which you manage someone who is dealing with a Q1 situation, have you:

- Assigned clear priority to the situation?
- Ascertained that there is enough time to accomplish the task?
- Provided appropriate training?
- Presented opportunity for the individual to gain experience?
- Made available the requisite levels of support?

If you can answer "yes" to these questions but are still seeing an individual demonstrate recurring Q1 behavior, then you have a decision to make. As a leader, you must take action on removing this individual or allowing him or her more time to fulfill his or her potential. It's an artful call. You need to gauge how constant the behavior is versus how quickly you need to intervene. Q1 behavior is corrosive and eats up time. While giving a person "one more" chance is tempting, in the long run, doing so is often imprudent. READY Thinkers have the common sense to expedite themselves and their organizations out of quadrant 1.

Quadrant 2: Proactive Humility

Quadrant 2 of the READY Thinking Accountability Matrix reflects those times when you have caused an issue but do not have the primary responsibility to solve it. Note that I say "primary responsibility." You always play a very important role in quadrant 2: anywhere from being a contributor on a team to being asked (or told) to stand clear of the work entirely.

At times in our professional or personal lives, we cause a problem but have to rely upon someone else to clean up our mess. It happens to us all. Even Hall of Fame athletes have to rely on their teammates to get them out of a jam from time to time. Tony-winning performers flub their cues on occasion, causing their cast mates to improvise on stage. CEOs say and do things that require others—generally those lower on the organization chart—to engage in damage control.

Situations in quadrant 2 can feel embarrassing and dishonoring. A problem we caused is out in the open and needs more than just a personal response. By definition, it necessitates communal involvement. Competent people don't like being in Q2.

Tackling issues in quadrant 2—I caused the problem, but someone else has to solve it—requires "proactive humility."

READY THINKING ACCOUNTABILITY MATRIX

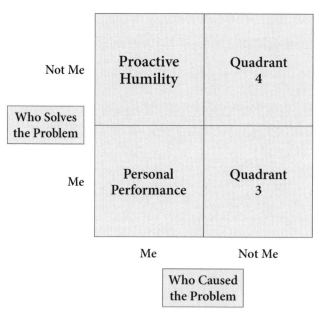

Humility is the quality of being grounded. It has a wonderful root in the Latin word "humus," meaning "ground" or "soil." It is the demonstration of respect and deference toward other people. It is the quality of modesty and unpretentiousness.

Not a lot of résumés highlighting a candidate's humility come across managers' desks:

"Dear Sir or Madam, I think I would fit well within your organization as I am dutifully aware of my shortcomings and have a lack of pride that allows me to affect a humble and self-depreciating style."

Nope.

More likely, the self-promoting qualities that we feel best improve our chances of getting a new job or a promotion are the opposites of humility: pride, aggressiveness, a take-charge attitude. We like our leaders to display a certain swagger. Meekness? Not for me. That sounds too much like a loser.

Displaying humility is dangerous. We connect it very closely to the worst of all outcomes: humiliation. But the two couldn't be further apart. The concept of humility is connected to strength, the ability to stay grounded, and the capacity to have a balanced perspective uncluttered by excess pride or hubris. Humble people exploit their strengths in part by recognizing their weaknesses and compensating for their failings.

Humiliation is another thing altogether. It is an act of degradation, synonymous with such things as disgrace and shame. While humiliation seems to have a wickedly sanctified place in our society (especially by those in the media), it has no place in our discussion about accountability.

Where humiliation edges into the worst of being human, humility is squarely at the center of what is best.

When you cause a problem and someone else has the responsibility to solve it, expressing humility is essential—not shame, which is paralyzing, and not defensiveness, which is distracting. Humility allows you to participate in finding the solution while acknowledging, with openness, your role in having caused the problem.

The first word "proactive" describing quadrant 2 of the READY Thinking Accountability Matrix shouldn't be overlooked. It means being demonstrative and declarative about the role you played in causing the problem and showing your willingness to play a role in resolving it, even if that role is to get out of the way and be a bystander.

Proactive humility is not an act of self-flagellation, although a self-effacing style provides many benefits. Proactive humility isn't a demonstration of how sorry you are, although a contrite manner is very helpful. Proactive humility isn't an exercise in self-doubt. It is an exercise to get to an answer and to move forward.

To achieve proactive humility, you must do three things overtly:

1. You must acknowledge your role in causing the issue.
2. You must apologize.
3. You must offer your assistance in resolving the issue.

Prepare for a Two-Minute Drill.

TWO-MINUTE DRILL
PROACTIVE HUMILITY

It's calendar time. Open your calendar and study the way you have used your time during the past week. Recall a situation where you found yourself in quadrant 2 of the READY Thinking Accountability Matrix: a situation that you—not to be indelicate—screwed up and where someone else had to clean up your mess.

What was the situation? _____

_____

Who was the individual (or team) that had the primary responsibility of correcting the situation?

_____

_____

Now, say the following to that individual (or team):

1. I admit/acknowledge my role in causing the problem.
2. I apologize.
3. I am here to help. What do you want me to do?

The alternative to proactive humility is wasted time and energy, the antithesis of READY Thinking.

PAUL IS A Q2 READY THINKER

A client was so livid with her account representative, Paul, that she threatened, in no uncertain terms, to immediately take her business elsewhere if she were ever to talk to him again. Paul didn't think that her experience warranted the level of outrage being demonstrated, but his opinion was beside the point. He had to quickly demonstrate Q2 behavior. He acknowledged that he caused this issue with the client and apologized to the team, and then he volunteered to assist in any way possible.

The time for defensiveness ("What I did wasn't so bad; it's not like this mistake hasn't been made before") or combativeness ("The client is being unreasonable—tell her to stick it") wasn't practicable.

continues ➤

113

> Paul played a key role in the service recovery. No one knew more about the client than he did, and without his help, it would have been impossible for his firm to reach an agreeable outcome with the client. Behind the scenes, Paul worked diligently to establish a service recovery plan, while others took the direct and face-to-face lead with the client.
>
> The team knew that next time, the roles might be reversed. That's the way it works.

Quadrant 3: Compassionate Command

Quadrant 3 is the reverse of the situation in Q2. Someone else caused a problem, and you have the primary role in resolving it.

Been there?

At the beginning of this chapter, I mentioned that being accountable had very little to do with fairness, and quadrant 3 of the READY Thinking Accountability Matrix is the most unfair of them all. Quadrant 3 issues can make you feel like someone is sticking it to you.

How many times have you heard yourself say, "Here we go: another mess for me to clean up." "How could they let this happen?" "Did they do that again? Now I'm left holding the bag."

Every job has a certain component that requires problem resolution. Quadrant 3 is something different: it holds the expectation of magnanimous performance over and above the typical duties of your job. Q3 issues elicit highly charged emotions that complicate your job and life: emotions such as anger, disillusionment, and, in extreme cases, hopelessness.

Being a READY Thinker doesn't mean you're unemotional. READY Thinkers are passionate and get duly angry or elated, as the situation warrants. No one wants to follow a robot, but, then again, no one wants to follow an emotional basket case either. There is a fine line between displaying emotions and becoming a victim to them.

Quadrant 3 requires the best of us because this quadrant presents the greatest challenge to accountability. It is tempting to succumb to the blame game; it is easy to feel righteous and retreat indignantly to moral high ground.

But, none of this wins the day. These behaviors don't demonstrate READY Thinking. It is reasonable to expect that we have to take some time to cool off and let negative emotions leach themselves out of us, but the READY Thinker does this faster than his or her competition.

Quadrant 3 of the READY Thinking Accountability Matrix requires taking command of the situation. Q3 situations require someone to firmly establish order and take control. They require action.

Finding yourself in a Q3 situation is analogous to being a member of the cavalry and being called upon to act with dispatch. We cannot hesitatingly stand on the ridge and merely overlook a bad situation, too transfixed to move. It is not the time to form a steering committee or send out long-winded e-mails. No! We must act. We must confront the situation with alacrity. It is a duty not lightly taken, but if you're part of the cavalry, then your role is clear. If you're not a member, then get off your high horse and get out of the way because you're confusing the situation.

Command is one attribute of Q3 behavior, but it is not enough. The second attribute is compassion. Without compassion, command is seen as insensitive and offensive. It is braying and loud. It creates downstream resentments and splits teams. Command without compassion aggravates Q3 situations by fanning the flames of begrudgement.

Compassion, the ability to hold sympathy for the perspective of others while maintaining a strong motivation for action, is a powerful attribute of a leader. Concern alone is not enough. Empathy with someone's situation is inadequate. The READY Thinker seeks to understand the situation, be sympathetic to all parties concerned, and be compelled to act.

Quadrant 3 situations call for compassionate command.

READY THINKING ACCOUNTABILITY MATRIX

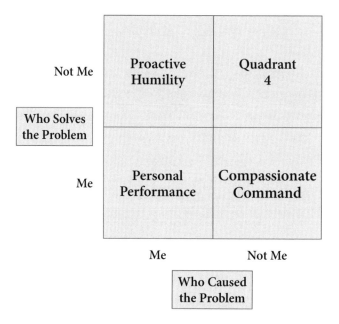

Hopefully, on the other side of this transaction is a READY Thinker who is practicing proactive humility. That makes the job a lot easier. Regardless, when someone else causes a problem and it's your role to solve it, conscious action delivered with urgency and compassion is required.

Prepare for a Two-Minute Drill.

TWO-MINUTE DRILL
COMPASSIONATE COMMAND

It's calendar time. Open your calendar and study the way you have used your time during the past week. Recall a quadrant 3 situation where you found your innocent self confronted with the task of cleaning up somebody else's mess.

What was the situation? _____

_____

Who was the individual (or team) that caused the situation?

_____

How did you react to the situation?_____

_____

How did you feel about the person or people causing this problem?

_____

Were you able to take command of the situation?
How did you do this?

_____

_____

continues ➤

117

Did you demonstrate compassion? How?

_____

_____

_____

Looking back, what could you have done differently to be more effective in demonstrating Q3 behavior?

_____

_____

_____

HARRY TRUMAN WAS
A Q3 READY THINKER

Harry S. Truman entered the presidency during the closing stages of one of the most destructive wars in world history. In a matter of a few months, this onetime haberdasher from Independence, Missouri, presided over the end of the war in Europe, ushered the world into the atomic age by dropping bombs on Hiroshima and Nagasaki (a bomb that during his time as vice president he was unaware even existed), created the Marshall Plan, dealt with treasonlike behavior from one of the country's most decorated and popular generals, supported the creation of a Jewish homeland, dealt with a massive and potentially debilitating strike from the railroad union, and the list goes on.

Here is what Truman said the day after FDR died, when he became president of the United States: "Boys, if you pray, pray for me now. I don't know whether you fellows ever had a load of hay fall on you, but when they told me yesterday what had happened, I felt like the moon and stars and all the planets had fallen on me."

As a means to remind himself (and his guests) of the president's job description, on one of his first days in the Oval Office, he placed a plaque on his desk that read "The buck stops here."

chapter 11

Quadrant 4 of the READY Thinking Accountability Matrix

"It is not necessary to my happiness."

I'm thrilled that you've made it this far into the book. Maybe a little surprised. Congratulations to both of us! I hope you've enjoyed it so far and have gotten something out of it. If not, just keep reading. The secret I share below has the power to immediately increase your productivity by—get this—25%!

You read that right.

You'll find yourself able to boost your effectiveness, generate more throughput, and heighten your personal impact in dramatic fashion. All naturally, no banned substances involved.

Here's the secret: quadrant 4 of the READY Thinking Accountability Matrix is **100% wasted time**.

People who spend time on issues they neither caused nor have a legitimate role in solving are wasting their time. Oh, the rationalizations:

"I'm curious about what's going on."

"I have opinions to share."

"I want to give feedback."

"I pride myself on staying in the loop."

"I have knowledge that others will want to tap into."

"Just put me on the distribution list; I'll attend if I can."

"I want to be part of the committee."

"My group needs to be represented on the team."

Or the classic, "E-mail me the information."

The READY Thinking Accountability Matrix is very clear. Quadrant 4 behavior is wasted time spent on problems you neither caused nor have a legitimate role in solving. What's the definition of having a legitimate role in solving a problem? Either you are a decision maker or you have a responsibility to take some kind of remedial action.

Expressing an opinion is not—I repeat *not*—in and of itself a legitimate role in solving a problem. I recognize that this is hard to accept. Your opinions are important. You have come to believe that providing your perspective is a divine right. You have bought into the idea that your viewpoint is welcomed—no, make that, *cherished*—by those around you.

Maybe what you've experienced isn't interest but misplaced politeness. Have you ever entertained the notion that people listen to you simply because they don't know how to tell you to zip it? It's not often you hear an opinion that matters from someone who neither caused the situation nor has a legitimate role in solving it.

People say that they are swamped by their workloads, that they feel stressed out and overwhelmed by the hours they put into their jobs. This isn't hard to imagine, given the amount of time that people spend in quadrant 4.

Too busy? Stop going to quadrant 4 meetings.

Taking work home at night? Stop spending time in quadrant 4 during the day.

Frustrated by your workload? Cut out the Q4.

Not spending enough quality time with friends and family? Stop Q4 lollygagging.

You want to practice READY Thinking? Get ruthless. When asked to attend a meeting, or participate in a project, or join a committee, ask yourself: Did I have a role in causing the problem being addressed? Do I have a legitimate role in solving it?

You'd be surprised at how often your answers will be "no." In fact, as you look at the people in your life whom you see as "successful," notice how often they say "no." Notice how cold-blooded they are about protecting their time and avoiding quadrant 4. Quadrant 4 requires you to *mind your own business.*

Pretty simple.

Mind your own business. Sometimes, at moments of great frustration, mind your own *freaking* business. But, generally, MYOB will suffice.

READY Thinking Accountability Matrix

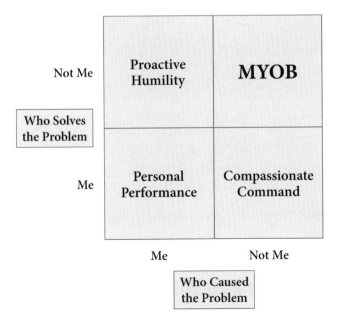

No way, you say. That's it? That's your big 25% productivity tip? I want my money back!

But, hold on there. If you've never exercised quadrant 4 READY Thinking, you have no idea how powerful it is.

Let's role-play:

Dick: I was thinking about attending that (meeting, committee, offsite, project kickoff, etc.) this afternoon.

Jane (Dick's leader):   I didn't know you had a role there. Did you cause the (problem/issue/gap/error/etc.)?

Dick: No, but I want to hear what is going on.

Or . . .

No, but I got the (invitation/meeting notice/e-mail/ heads-up).

Jane: Do you have a legitimate role in solving the (problem/issue/situation/gap/error)?

Dick: Well, not a direct role. But, my opinion could be helpful. I have had a lot of experience with this sort of thing throughout the years.

Jane: Dick, you've been complaining recently about (the long hours you're putting in at the office/taking work home/ stress due to tight deadlines/all of the above).

I think it would be better **if you minded your own business and didn't waste time** in that meeting.

Dick: Excellent feedback, Jane.

Thanks for the coaching. I guess I'll use my time this afternoon to get those month-end reports done so that I don't have to take them home this weekend. Thanks for the great leadership.

Let's face it: unless Dick's last name is Gandhi, he'll likely get his nose bent out of shape for being told by his leader (or anyone, for that matter) to mind his own business. It is exactly what he needs to hear, but he won't like it. Telling someone to "MYOB" in today's society is pretty far up there in the pantheon of interpersonal sins.

So here is what Jane says:

Jane: Dick, you've been complaining recently about (the long hours you're putting in at the office/taking work home/ stress due to tight deadlines/all of the above).

I think it would be better to avoid what I see as quadrant 4 behavior.

Remember the READY Thinking Accountability Matrix: you neither caused the problem nor have a legitimate role in solving it.

I think it would be better if you maintained Q4 discipline in regard to spending your time in that meeting.

Prepare for a Two-Minute Drill.

Two-Minute Drill

Role Playing

It's calendar time. Open your calendar and study the way you have used your time during the past week. Recall a situation where you interacted with someone who was in quadrant 4 of the READY Thinking Accountability Matrix. This individual was assertive in expressing an opinion about the subject or problem at hand but neither caused the issue nor had a legitimate role in solving it.

Who was this person? _____

_____

What was the situation? _____

_____

_____

Now, say the following to that individual:

"_____, I realize you have an opinion about _____. When I look at the situation, though, I cannot see where you caused the problem or what role you have in solving it. _____, I'm going to let you mind your own business."

Example:

"**MOM**, I realize you have an opinion about **HOW I DISCIPLINE MY KIDS**. When I look at the situation, though, I cannot see where you caused the problem or what role you have in solving it. **MOM**, I'm going to let you mind your own business."

There are people we work with (live with/coach with/are friends with/are related to) who whip out personal opinions like switchblades. They think everything is fair game. They stumble around in a Q4 fog and toss their perspectives at you with the practiced nonchalance of a circus knife thrower. They carpet bomb with judgments. Are they in quadrant 4? They define it. The amount of time taken to beat back their asides, listen to their soliloquies, deflect their input, and disperse their negligibility is enormous. And every minute, every second, is wasted effort.

Prepare for a Two-Minute Drill.

TWO-MINUTE DRILL
MYOB

Once again, it's calendar time. Open your calendar and study the way you have used your time during the past business week. The first step of this drill is to identify those blocks of time you have spent dealing with issues (A) that you didn't cause and (B) that you had no legitimate role (i.e., you were not the decision maker, and you had no tasks to complete) in solving. These are Q4 situations.

Be ruthless in your analysis. Avoid rationalizing your involvement in these Q4 issues. Notice how much time is being spent in

continues ➤

this quadrant. Say to yourself, "This was wasted time. This was misused energy. This was a part of my day that I squandered."

Q4 situations can be prevented. It takes practice and backbone. As you look out to the next five business days, establish an action plan to eliminate the amount of time you intend to spend on Q4 situations.

You now have found extra time on your calendar—perhaps as much as *25%* of your schedule has been freed up! What will you do?

- Make that extra sales call
- Finish that project you've been putting off
- Complete the work you were going to take home this weekend
- Take a class at your local university
- Volunteer at Meals on Wheels
- Be a room parent at your kid's school

Spend two minutes contemplating how you would spend an extra five to 10 hours a week in your life, and write the response here:

_____

_____

_____

When your resolve weakens, when doubt creeps into your decision making and you find yourself struggling with cutting out Q4 situations from your weekly activities, reinforce your determination by reading what you wrote above.

Recognizing when you are in quadrant 4 is one of the most liberating experiences you can have in life. It allows you a rare and legitimate opportunity to "let go" and "let others."

It doesn't come without a cost. Minding your own business can make you seem standoffish or not a team player. Early in your career, especially, you can have a sense of not being as well networked as the next person. You run the risk, as remote as it is, that some plum assignment will get tossed to a contemporary who is less deserving.

But have faith. Knowing when to mind your own business is a talent that will pay off handsomely. You will find more time in your day, better focus, and a calmness that others find reassuring. The people around you will see a leader who is in command of himself or herself.

ELSA EINSTEIN WAS A Q4 READY THINKER

Relativity is easy: the fundamental laws of physics are the same whatever your state of motion. Albert Einstein introduced the theory of relativity in 1905 and explained, "It is a theory of space and time as far as physics is concerned, which leads to the theory of gravitation." Whatever. His theory both shocked and startled the world. It led to surprising conclusions: $E=MC^2$, time dilation, relativity of simultaneity, the existence of black holes, and length contraction. At its core is the replacement of Galilean transformations of classical mechanics with Lorentz transformations.

The brilliant biochemist Chaim Weizman made a transatlantic crossing with Einstein during which Einstein tried to explain relativity. Weizman said, "During the crossing, Einstein explained his theory to me every day, and by the time we arrived, I was

continues ➤

fully convinced that he really understands it." Philip Lenard, a Nobel laureate, labeled Einstein's theory "absurd." The U.S. Senate debated whether to record Einstein's theories in the Congressional Record but found them unfathomable.

When asked whether she understood the theory, Albert's wife, Elsa, replied, "Oh, no, although he explained it to me several times. But, it is not necessary to my happiness."

The D in READY
Thinking: Durability

"Every painful event contains in itself a seed of growth and liberation."

D urability—the ability to stick with something through good times and bad, victory and heartbreak, happy emotions and sad—is the most powerful attribute a READY Thinker can have. Period.

It is stronger than talent.

It is better than luck.

It is more real than potential.

It is more valuable than intellect.

Durability is better than all these things combined.

Durability is the value that has delivered to you every good thing in your life. In *The Way to Love*, Tony de Mello writes:

Think of some of the painful events in your life. For how many of them are you grateful today, because thanks to them you changed and grew? Here is the simple truth of life that most people never discover. Happy events make life delightful but they do not lead to self-discovery and growth and freedom. That privilege is reserved to the things and persons and situations that cause us pain.

What a peculiar way of thinking about things that cause us pain. Privileges? That takes some getting used to.

As I was doing research for this book, I happened to speak to an acquaintance who had unexpectedly lost his lucrative corporate job at the same time his wife was going through chemotherapy in a battle against cancer. In addition, during this period, his son was in a 90-day inpatient treatment program for chemical dependency. I thought this situation was horribly sad and asked how he was holding up.

Here is what he said: "I feel incredibly blessed. My son was very close to killing himself with his substance abuse. He never would have allowed himself to be admitted into treatment, save for the fact that his mother was so terribly sick. In fact, he awoke one night after a nightmare where he had dreamt his mother was calling out to him for help, but he was too wasted to come to her aid. The next morning he got himself admitted.

"With her son in treatment, my wife had someone to worry about besides herself. She used this to avoid becoming self-absorbed with her disease. She felt that being involved with her son's recovery enabled her to more willingly accept her own treatment regimen.

"As for me, watching my family suffer through these trials really put my job search into perspective. I decided to focus on finding a new career that was truly meaningful and not allow myself to take the next job just out of panic and desperation. Where I would have likely seen losing my job as a great betrayal and personal loss, witnessing what was going on with my wife and my son and the courage they were demonstrating, I decided

I would take the perspective that losing my job was a great opportunity for me to find something to do that I felt passionate about."

This was not what I thought I was going to hear from this man. It struck me that for the first time in a long time, I heard peace and calmness in his voice. Life had roughed up him and his family pretty badly. I expected that he would have been bitter and resentful. On the contrary, he was wholeheartedly facing the tribulations of his life with great dignity.

Three key elements empowered this man with resiliency:

- Faith: He believed that the journey was important and that, in the end, things would work out for the best.
- Forgiveness: He held no crippling, self-limiting acrimony.
- Family (or Friends): He was surrounded with love and support. He was not in this struggle alone.

Gordon MacDonald, author of the book *A Resilient Life*, describes resilient people as those "who have gotten healthier as life has gone on in every sense of the word. They generally are people who somewhere along the line have gone through various forms of adversity, have not only survived it, but thrived in the middle of it."

Durability also requires a fourth element, discipline: the ability to control your own behavior and impulses. Durable people practice willpower. They display fortitude and grit. They accomplish the goals in their lives with determination.

Harry Truman said, "In reading the lives of great men, I found that the first victory they won was over themselves . . . self discipline with all of them came first."

Self-will is the precursor to accomplishment.

People would much rather hear about the preternatural career trajectory than the ordinary one, but the "secret" of career advancement lies far less in shrewd and prescient career moves than it does in the discipline to show up ready to work every day.

It is seldom recognized that an artist's glory is tethered more closely to the ability to operate when discouraged than it is to artistic ability. A healthy marriage is often romanticized as one where you "find your soul mate" or "complete each other." But, a solid, happy, enduring marriage is mostly about developing the discipline to deal with the day-to-day ups and downs of living your life with someone else.

Asked the one key ability he desired in his football players—Speed? Quickness? Strength?—Bud Grant, the legendary head coach of the Minnesota Vikings, responded: "Durability."

Prepare for a Two-Minute Drill.

TWO-MINUTE DRILL
POWER OF PURPOSE

A durable person has a sense of purpose. Setbacks come and go, hindering our progress, but the big picture remains. Considering our purpose is essential because it energizes us when the chips are down. We see the journey as important because it moves us to a bigger and more expansive goal. We can endure the hardship because we think it will be worthwhile.

What is the purpose of your life? _____

_____

To achieve this purpose, what are your imperatives, the things that are absolutely necessary and unavoidable?

_____

_____

What are the things keeping you from fully realizing your purpose?

_____

_____

This is a huge question to consider. It might take more than two minutes.

You can break this drill down and do the same exercise on individual parts of your life: marriage, parenting, friendship, etc. Below is an example:

What is the purpose of your marriage? **To enjoy the passage of time, raise two healthy, well-adjusted children, grow in deeper faith and understanding of God's work in our life . . .**

To achieve this purpose, what are your imperatives, the things that are absolutely necessary and unavoidable? **Spending time with my wife, honesty, mutual respect and fidelity, prayer, shared vision of our lives together, laughter, living under consistent values . . .**

What are the things keeping you from fully realizing your marriage's purpose? **Time pressure, too many things on the calendar, too much financial stress, lack of compromise . . .**

In doing this exercise, you are creating the discipline to stay focused on the big picture in your life, to put that first, and to remind yourself why you are in a marriage, a career, a parental commitment, etc. When the inevitable obstacles arise or misfortune hampers your progress, it's good to know what you are trying to accomplish and why it's important.

WINSTON CHURCHILL WAS A READY THINKER

Winston Churchill was one of the most important leaders in history. His strategic brilliance turned the tide of the war with the Axis. His speeches provided inspiration to millions of embattled Brits. He was an outspoken, but largely ignored, voice against seeking appeasement with Germany, and he watched in horror the rise of Adolph Hitler and the Nazis. To no avail, he pushed the government to take hard steps to strengthen its resolve in response to Hitler's growing power—a failing he held himself accountable for until the day he died.

In the early days of WWII, he advocated for preemptive strikes against key strategic targets to deny the Germans territory and resources, only to watch helplessly as both the British prime minister and the rest of the War Cabinet dithered and debated. Germany invaded Poland and then Norway, the Netherlands, Belgium, and France. The Nazi invasion of Great Britain appeared to be imminent. All seemed lost, but Churchill refused to capitulate to the idea of defeat and surrender. Few of his contemporaries could muster such conviction.

> *"We shall defend our island, whatever the cost may be, we shall fight on the beaches, we shall fight on the landing grounds, we shall fight on the fields and in the streets, we shall fight in the hills; we shall never surrender . . . Let us therefore brace ourselves to our duties, and so bear ourselves that, if the British Empire and its Commonwealth last*

for a thousand years, they will still say, 'This was their finest hour.'"

Churchill spent nearly 60 years in public service as a statesman and soldier. He won the Nobel Prize. He was one of the modern world's most inspirational orators. He kept democracy's flame burning in Britain while there were serious world doubts about turning back the seemingly invincible Nazi war machine. Without him, there would be no Normandy invasion, no liberation of France, no victory in Europe, no blunting of the Soviet influence in Western Europe.

A few months after VE Day, perhaps the most validating day of his life, Churchill lost his bid for reelection to a landslide victory by the opposing party.

Think it was easy for him to go to work the next morning? He did get up, and he did go back to work. Six years later, he was reelected to the position of prime minister.

Our society has evolved to a point where we try to protect our kids from all bad news. We hold sporting competitions without keeping score. We grade on relative ability. We insist that everyone gets equal playing time. We intervene when a teacher or coach evaluates our kids below what we think is fair. We heap praise on the slightest achievement and overkill it on the self-esteem.

But life isn't like that. Success comes from effort. Life is filled with setbacks and failure. Sometimes there is bad luck. It is all too tempting to get beaten down and refuse to rise once again. No doubt our careers, our friendships, and even our marriages can become a real grind. Our culture promises immediate fulfillment. *Not happy? Go spend some money, take somebody to court, eat that pan of brownies, take a hit, have a drink.*

I'm sorry to say so
But, sadly, it's true
That Bang-ups
And Hang-ups
Can happen to you.

You can get all hung up
In a prickle-ly perch.
And your gang will fly on.
You'll be left in a Lurch.

—Dr. Seuss
Oh, the Places You'll Go

The opposite of durability is aimlessness: drifting from one thing to the next. Aimless lives get built unintentionally. We wake up and wonder what we did with our youth. Where did the time go? What do I have to show for it?

Durable people have learned to focus on what they can control. They see pressure as a chance to seek advantage, obstacles as a way to find openings. Being durable doesn't mean you don't fail; it just means you can collect yourself after a setback and focus on the next step—however small it might be—despite feeling disappointed and anxious. Ralph Waldo Emerson wrote, "Our greatest glory consists not in never falling but rather in rising when we fall."

You may be discouraged that the ultimate goals seem so impossible and that the challenge is insurmountable. But taking just one little step puts you back on the path to achieving goals that seem unattainable.

Mother Teresa, when asked how she came to be regarded as the most powerful woman in the world, simply replied, "Small work done with great love."

Prepare for a Two-Minute Drill.

TWO-MINUTE DRILL
VISUALIZING SUCCESS

Learn to visualize success and only success. Eliminate the corrosive practice of rehashing failure or depressing events in your life. Visualize success first by calming your mind. Recall an episode in your life that was truly outstanding. In great detail evoke the episode. For example, perhaps it was winning a golf tournament. Take yourself mentally back to that event. Drill down into the detail. Focus on one shot you made that was especially memorable. What club was in your hand? Who was around you? How green was the grass? Which way was the wind blowing? What did you smell? How did the ball come off the clubface? Where did the divot fly? How high was the ball in the air? How long was the ball in the air? Visualize how the ball landed on the putting surface. What did your hear?

Suck up the feeling you experience like a sponge. Feel it oozing in your body, coming out of your pores.

The durable person will take this feeling into the next challenge, use it as a power of suggestion, call upon it in times of doubt, and recall every little detail to refresh a sense of confidence and security.

The companies you prefer to give your business to, the people you like to surround yourself with, the leaders you like to work for—they all have had to endure some bad times. They have used their trials to become changed, inevitably for the better. They have developed character and integrity; during hard times, you trust that they'll have your back.

Durability has an interesting physical component: it requires both emotional and physical stamina. The strength of your resilience is tied to your vigor. If you struggle with finding time to add exercise and proper diet into your daily life, remember that they add fortitude that links directly to your READY Thinking.

We recognize when people have a strong inner core. These people reflect a faith that provides them a prodigious resilience and stamina. My Grandma Emma was one of these people.

GRANDMA EMMA WAS
A READY THINKER

Grandma Emma had six children, losing one at childbirth and another later in life. The second-to-youngest was my mother. Emma lived through tumultuous and troubling times: two world wars, the Great Depression, and an untold number of personal trials, including being married to a man who suffered Alzheimer's (back when it was called "old-age disease") for the last 15 years of their marriage. She once said that during the Depression, she had to choose between burning corn to heat her home or cooking it to feed her children.

Which puts the deliberation as to whether to give our 13-year-old a cell phone into perspective.

Despite all life had to throw at her, she remained upbeat and resolute to the end. Her posture was twisted by osteoporosis, but her faith, her inclination to see the goodness of life, remained unbent.

She was of that generation that seldom sat still. There always was one more thing to get done. But, once in a while out on the porch, under the big apple tree—after dinner had been caught, plucked, cooked, and served and after the pots had been washed, the table cleared, and the dishes put away—she listened with care to the naive and shallow complaints of overindulged grandchildren, looked over her glasses, and said something like, "You'll be fine; just do what fills your basket" or "Don't worry yourself about that; it's not worth weeds in the garden."

She never interrupted. She was never condescending or judgmental. She'd simply listen with focus. Of course, advice coming from a woman who had experienced and overcome so much in her life came as if from the burning bush: a reassuring balm for a confused soul.

Durability bestows credibility. Grandma Emma had a standing in life that was rooted in authenticity and trustworthiness. Who wants to listen to, let alone follow, someone who is untested? Someone who hasn't experienced both the tops and the bottoms of the cycles in life?

So when is it time to stop enduring? It is true: sometimes things are not worth enduring. A degrading relationship, a duplicitous partner, or an abusive marriage can be unendurable. Working for an unethical boss, or with a team you cannot trust, or in a corrupt company—these are situations that call for judiciousness and wisdom.

When endurance leads to the compromise of your personal core ethics, then it is time to separate. Compromising your core values leads to disconnectedness. Your body starts doing something your mind and spirit cannot support. This accelerates an energy drain that leads to disengagement. Durability is all about staying involved. Hard times, bad times, they can make you stronger—but not at a cost to the self.

Granted, suffering is unsettling. Bad things happen to good people. It would be great to eliminate "D is for Durability" in READY Thinking and expect never to suffer through pain and setback. Apparently, it just doesn't work that way. Good times come, and good times go. There are times when you can't but win and other times you think the slump will never end. There are times when the city is electrifying with its culture and glory and other times when evil people destroy buildings, take innocent lives, and leave us feeling horribly insecure. READY Thinkers see both as basic elements of life.

> *Some folks say, that I've got the perfect life,*
> *Three swell kids, lots of toys and a lovely wife.*

> *I fly, I sail, I throw caution to the wind,*
> *Drift like a stratus cloud above the Caribbean,*

> *But, every now and then,*
> *The dragons come to call.*

> *Just when you least expect it,*
> *You'll be dodging cannon balls . . .*

> —*Jimmy Buffet*
> *"Jamaica Mistaica"*
> *From his album* Banana Wind

For a while, I suppose, you can fake yourself through it. You can take pains to jump ship at just the right time. Connive to avoid being blamed for a failure. Work only on the path of least resistance. Never stick your neck out. Never struggle. Never fail. Never fall. Never build endurance.

And, never be ready.

In his book *Ethics for the New Millennium*, His Holiness the Dalai Lama writes:

> *It is . . . worth remembering that the time of greatest gain in terms of wisdom and inner strength is often that of greatest difficulty.*
>
> *We can simply fret about our misfortunes. But, when we do so, we become frustrated. As a result . . . our peace of mind is destroyed. When we do not restrain our tendency to react negatively to suffering, it becomes a source of negative*

thoughts and emotions. There is thus a clear relationship between the impact suffering has on our heart and mind and our practice of inner discipline.

Unfortunate events, though potentially a source of anger and despair, have equal potential to be a source of spiritual growth. Whether or not this is the outcome depends on our response.

Or, as Winston Churchill more bluntly put it, "If you are going through hell, keep going."

chapter 13

The Y in READY
Thinking: YES! Outlook

*"How you think of a fact may defeat you
before you can do anything about it."*

If you're not careful, you can have a whole lot of fun in this life.

You'd never know it by watching most people, but it's the truth.

Life can be a hoot.

Some people don't believe this. No place is this more evident than at our jobs. Some people refuse to enjoy their work, while others enjoy their work but refuse to show it. That's a real shame because one of the things positive people find most rewarding about life is engaging with other positive people. One of the things people find most rewarding about their jobs is the talent and passion of the people they work with.

Where is it written that we must act overburdened, overwrought, and overworked and constantly look harried? What section of the employee manual dictates that employees have to be miserable? Who mandated that the question "How's it going?" requires the exasperated reply "I'm really busy"?

Having fun and enjoying your work pays dividends. Having a positive attitude is contagious. People—friends, coworkers, clients—want to be part of the energy. They are attracted to the optimism and confidence.

Get on the bandwagon!

Why do fans support a winning team and not a losing one? It's going to the ballpark expecting success. It's the feeling that even when confronted with a tough situation (bases loaded, nobody out), our guys will find a way out of the jam. You're part of the excitement and a member of the team.

Why do customers buy your product or service? They want a positive experience. They have a choice, and they want to choose a winner. They want you to help them achieve their goals as part of their team.

People want success. They want to win. They want to have optimism and faith in the outcome. They want to enjoy themselves.

Having a "YES!" outlook is not a luxury. Negative attitudes beget negative outcomes. The cycle of negativity spirals down on itself; it becomes a failure loop. Who wants to be part of that? As the saying goes, no one ever erected a statue to a pessimist.

Your attitude is the first thing that distinguishes you to others. People pick up on your vibe in an instant. Your frame of mind triggers an emotional response in the first split seconds of an encounter. This can be attributed to our adaptive unconscious, the ability to form a notion of what another thinks and thinks about what we are thinking. It is an advantageous skill, honed through the evolution of our species, providing the handy ability to predict the way others will respond. Our adaptive unconscious targets the cues that another is emitting: cues such as facial expressions, body language, breathing patterns, nonverbal pauses, and other such stimuli.

This skill, sometimes called intuition or ESP, works to a degree in all of us. In his book *Blink*, Malcom Gladwell writes about the theory of "thin slicing." Thin slicing deals with rapid cognition, the ability of the human subconscious to find patterns in situations and behavior based on very narrow slices of experience. Gladwell observes that in sports, we say an athlete can "see the whole field"; in the military, we praise the general who possesses "coup d'oeil," or the "power of a glance," the ability to immediately see and make sense of the battlefield.

If you move through life with a negative attitude, the theory of thin slicing argues that others will instantly pick up subtle signs of your pessimism or defeatism. Imagine the damage to your effectiveness if over the course of many years, the first impression people got from you was vaguely sour. Perhaps not from anything you said or didn't say—or anything overtly negative you did—but your negative attitude would nonetheless create tremors of uncertainty and cautiousness.

Compare this way of moving through life with a positive outlook, where others, consciously or unconsciously, are drawn to your pluck and ambition. They sense your zest for life and your sincere optimism and are naturally attracted to it and want to be part of it.

Compounded over time and multiple experiences, these minute deviations in how others behave toward you can make the difference between living a successful, impactful life or one filled with frustrations, setbacks, and regrets.

What was it that attracted us to our mate? How do we choose the best employee from a group of equally qualified candidates? What attracts us to the people we have as friends? How do we choose what doctor to trust, or who to handle our finances, or a nanny for our children?

You've said it yourself: sometimes it just clicks; sometimes it doesn't. It is hard to always explain why. Generally, though, we have been attracted to people who have emitted an aura of optimism. They are confident, they like who they are, they like what they do, and they project a positive energy.

They aren't always positive—they have their share of down days too—but, in general, their natural disposition is to say "YES!" to life.

No doubt we need to take what we do very seriously—but that doesn't mean we have to take ourselves seriously. For crying out loud, life is short! We spend a lot of it (some estimate 60% of our adult waking life) at work. Let's enjoy it. People don't want to go to work and leave their crushed souls out in the car, careful to crack a window for ventilation. They connect with their work when they have alignment between their heads and their hearts. When heads and hearts are aligned, effort comes naturally, and the day flies by. Challenges are energetically confronted. Change is handled effortlessly.

When we cannot keep things in perspective, having a YES! outlook becomes difficult. The problems that we confront today can seem insurmountable. The volume of work before us may appear overwhelming.

Prepare for a Two-Minute Drill.

TWO-MINUTE DRILL
ESTABLISHING PERSPECTIVE

Consider the physical location you are in right now. It might be a chair in the library, a desk at school, or a reading place in your home. For purposes of this drill, let's say it's the office space you work in. Spend some time thinking about the problems that you will be dealing with out of this office today. This should be easy: it's probably those things you think you should be doing instead of reading this book. Write these things down and include a description of how the tasks make you feel. I've started for you.

Redo budget: *feels similar to redrilling a root canal*

_____

_____

_____

Now, think back to the problems you were dealing with in this office space at this time last week. Do they seem more or less intense than those issues you are dealing with today

_____

_____

_____

Go further back. Recall the problems being dealt with in this office space last year. You may be the one dealing with these problems, or maybe it was someone else who occupied your office space before you. Either way, what might the issues have been? Do they seem as important as what you are dealing with today?

_____

_____

_____

Still further. What were the problems being faced by the person sitting in your space five years ago? Maybe this person was you; maybe

continues ➤

it was someone else. What was this person feeling/what were you feeling? Were the issues real? Did they cause stress and anxiety? Go back 10 years.

_____

_____

_____

Now, go back 100 years. Maybe your office space wasn't in existence, perhaps not even the office building itself. But, imagine what was going on in the location of your existing office space 100 years ago. What might have been the issues? How did the people react? Were they overwhelmed?

_____

_____

_____

Imagine 10,000 years ago, 100,000 years ago, 1,000,000 years ago. What was going on?

_____

_____

_____

The earth is millions of years old. We're not the first ones to feel the pressure. Our generation didn't invent stress and strain; they've been companions throughout eons. Just as our ancestors survived, so do we. We have a hard time recalling what we were doing last month, let alone how we felt about it. The worry and anxiousness we felt last year is far too distant to recall.

Keeping things in perspective doesn't make the intensity of our emotions any less real; rather, it is a method of dealing with the intensity and making it less damaging. Stress can be a killer. There is nothing funny about it—which, I suppose, is why it can be a killer. We will never be stress free. It is always in us. We have to deal with it in some way, and maintaining perspective is a major tool we have at our disposal.

Prepare for a Two-Minute Drill.

TWO-MINUTE DRILL

ESTABLISHING PERSPECTIVE II

Do the same drill as above but look forward in time. What issues will you be dealing with in five years? Ten years? Do they seem as important as what you are dealing with today?

_____

_____

_____

Imagine that in 20 years, one of your children is sitting in this very spot. What will he or she be dealing with? Are his or her issues real? Is he or she feeling stress and anxiety? If you could magically speak to him or her, what would you want to say?

continues ➤

Imagine that in 100 years, one of your ancestors (a great-great-great grandchild) is sitting in this very spot. What will he or she be dealing with? Are his or her issues real? Is he or she feeling stress and anxiety? If you could magically speak to him or her, what would you want to say?

Imagine 10,000 years from now, 100,000 years from now, 1,000,000 years from now. What is going on?

Using the perspective of time is magic: you can begin to see that life is remarkably short and our worries and anxieties very fleeting. You will never be stress free, but you can live a life liberated from it. You have the ability to let it go and drain it of its power.

In the Bible (Matthew 6:25), Jesus says, "Therefore I tell you, do not be anxious about your life . . . look at the birds of the air . . . consider the lilies of the field." Stress is always about the past or the future. Nothing in the present is unbearable. Birds and flowers are stress free. They live in the now. So can you.

Consider the different types of stress: old stress is the stress we cling to, and new stress is the stress that can compel us to action and performance. It's the old stress that has us reaching for the nitroglycerin tablets. How long can you hold on to stress? A long time but not forever. Old stress is like holding up your hand full of marbles: despite the seemingly insignificant weight, eventually you reach a breaking point and the marbles spill out of your hand. They feel like bowling balls. Without some sort of relief, the marbles become too heavy for you to handle.

Emerson wrote, "A man is what he thinks about all day." Dwelling on old stress leaves you feeling pessimistic and despairing. If Emerson is right, your station in life will soon follow. Carry that thought around for a while. Talk about something too heavy to handle.

We need to find relief, but where to find it?

You've heard it before, *which doesn't make it less true*, but a YES! outlook is self-determined.

Having a YES! outlook is thinking with power. It is taking the time to fill your mind up with positive, optimistic energy. READY Thinkers visualize only things they want to have happen, so they visualize success. In no way does having a YES! outlook imply that we ignore our problems. We have to acknowledge the challenges in our lives, or they fester and grow into crises. Having a YES! outlook is facing the problem with a confident and positive posture. To some, the idea of being an optimist is the same as being naive to the facts. That's not true. In his book *The Power of Positive Thinking*, Norman Vincent Peale addresses this fallacy:

> *How you think of a fact may defeat you before you can do anything about it. You may permit a fact to overwhelm you*

153

mentally before you start to deal with it actually. On the other hand, a confident and optimistic thought pattern can modify or overcome the fact altogether.

To change your thinking, *you have to think differently.* If you are anxious and full of worry, behave in a petty manner, find yourself lashing out at minor discretions, and feel threatened and exhausted at the day's end, then you need to spend time filling up your mind with new and different things. But, first you must recognize that it's awfully crowded in that cranium of yours. You might want to clear some space.

Prepare for a Two-Minute Drill.

TWO-MINUTE DRILL

CENTERING

Clear your head and empty your mind. To do this, I want you to identify one area in your life currently causing you worry, anxiety, fear, and/or pain. Picture these emotions as real entities in your mind. Now, let them go. Relax and let these negative emotions and thoughts flow out of you like air out of a balloon. Relax and, with each exhalation, imagine your mind clearing itself of these limiting thoughts and emotions.

Say to yourself, "I now have peace. I now have tranquility."

Now visualize success. Fill yourself up with power. Once again, identify one area of your life where you are seeking strength and potency. With each inhalation, say the words "I believe." Focus on what you want and ask for it. Visualize filling your mind up with creative energy.

Say to yourself, "I am wholehearted. I am victorious. I intend to live with this spirit for the rest of the day."

Yes.

I know.

This can sound like a bunch of hooey. There are charlatans who claim you can think your way to great riches. Some of these folks go way too far, but I will give them this: you generally don't accomplish those things you think you can't. The first step is believing in yourself.

Developing a YES! outlook is a process requiring discipline. If you are not naturally inclined to having a positive outlook in life, you need to take well-thought-out steps to improve your attitude. On the one hand, you can try to stop thinking negative thoughts—but the very attention you bestow gives the negativity even more power. On the other, you can commit to thinking positive thoughts. You have to bring a YES! outlook to bear, not just when everything is going swimmingly but when things are tough, when the outlook is bleaker than you'd hope. It may start out as a chore, but drills (like the one above) move into a practice, and practice eventually turns into habit.

Prepare for a Two-Minute Drill.

TWO-MINUTE DRILL
POWER THINKING

Identify the things that fill up your mind during the day. If they are negative, then resolve to replace them with positive energy:

- The radio programs you listen to on the way into work. Buy a foreign-language course on tape and listen to it in the car. Next time someone asks how your commute was, simply say "Magnifico, grazi!"

continues ➤

- The nightly news. Stop filling your head with murder and mayhem right before you sleep. Turn the TV off. Read a historical novel or a Shakespearean comedy.
- Have PDA-free zones in your life. The thing does have an off button on it somewhere. Listen to inspirational music instead.
- Your e-mail. Take a moment right now and send yourself a message at work: "John, I think you're fantastic. Whatever is going to happen today, you can handle it. Good job!" Of course, you want to use your own name, not mine.
- Your voicemail. Next time you want to vent, have at it. Instead of calling someone to dump on, call your own voicemail. Call yourself and use your phone to voice *wail*. Then, take 24 hours to calm down and then check your message. You might be glad you vented to yourself.
- Have your son or daughter draw you pictures on a Post-It note. Stick these mini-Picassos on your dashboard, your computer screen, the whiteboard in the conference room, and the inside of your briefcase.

Other ideas:

_____

_____

_____

People charged with a positive mental attitude are magnetic. They attract attention and seem to exert a pull on others. They seem to be having more fun than the rest of us.

And, having fun is an exceptional way to live.

chapter 14

You Are a READY Thinker

"What are you going to do with your life?"

Under the apple tree, many years ago, Grandma Emma asked me a most remarkable question.

"So," she addressed me over the top of her glasses, "what are you going to do with your life?"

I had just graduated from the university and had no clue. I mumbled something about wanting to be a success, go make a lot of money, get a big-time job, stuff like that.

"I didn't ask whether you wanted to be successful," she gently chided. "Success in life comes once you know what you're living for. What are you going to do with your life?"

It was sort of a trick question—and one I have been trying to answer for 30 years. Success doesn't seem to be the endgame; it has, as Ben Franklin said, ruined many a man. It is nothing more, or less, than a label. It doesn't seem to be the thing to live for.

But, then, neither does failure.

Learning what to live for is the purpose of your time here on Earth.

NIKE, GODDESS OF VICTORY, IS A READY THINKER

Nike, Goddess of Victory, is represented by the statue of Winged Victory on display (dramatically on the sweeping Dura staircase) in the Louvre in Paris. Discovered in 1863 on the island of Samothrace, Greece, the statue by an unknown artist dates back to 200 BC and is considered a masterpiece.

Nike stands on the prow of some ancient vessel, encouraging its anonymous occupants forward. The figure's garments are windblown by strong ocean breezes. Age and travel have damaged the sculpture: only her torso and legs remain. Despite her injuries, or maybe because of them, her manner appears divine and offers breathtaking optimism. Wings fan out behind her; her body leans expectantly forward. Fearlessly, she confronts the future and calls for us to do the same.

You imagine the look in her eye, perhaps not unlike that of Michelangelo's *David*: composed, confident, and highly attentive but exultant as well. You envision her hair catching the wind as the gales of chance and opportunity blow hard against her. Her missing arms would surely be reaching out to grasp her destiny. She is an ancient symbol but one that speaks of triumph as impressively

---

today as she did 2,000 years ago. She stands in the most ready posture possible.

"Transform yourself," she seems to say. "Face reality. You can handle it.

"Enlarge yourself," she commands. "You are part of something bigger than the task at hand. Hold yourself to high levels of accountability. You are tough and durable. The journey may not be easy—after all, few worthwhile things in life are—but you can be joyful in your engagement of all that life has to offer."

Implicit in Grandma Emma's question "What will you do with your life?"—and inherent in the spirit behind the statue of *Nike*, expressed in the look in *David*'s eyes, underlying the great myth of Beowulf, ingrained in the soil of a Zen garden, and immanent in the writings of the mystics—is the irresistible call to find growth in our lives.

What is the miracle that generates growth? That miracle is change: a sharp stick of stimulus that leads us to do—what can seem to our minds—dangerous and scary things. Without it, we exist without truly living. **Not all change leads to growth, but all growth requires change.**

Many seek perfection by striving to eliminate the imperfection in their lives. This is called management. But, life isn't perfect. It can throw us curveballs, deal us misfortune and setback, derail our best-laid plans, and offer challenge and opportunity that we cannot today conceive. READY Thinkers seek perfection by incorporating life's imperfection, using five principles to take action—and find growth—when confronted by change:

- Reality
- Enlarging
- Accountability

- Durability
- YES! Outlook

Using these five principles can change your life: so start creating your best possible life today. Achieve higher performance levels, be more successful, win more often and teach others to do the same: You are a READY Thinker.

WHAT'S NEXT? How can I share the benefits of *READY Thinking* with others?

- Generate passion around the five principles of *READY Thinking*. Have the author speak to your group. John Baker is one of the country's leading speakers. His high-energy and engaging keynote presentation turns your next meeting or conference into a motivational and memorable event. People will be talking about John's address far into the future and using his principles in life-changing ways!

- Engage clients. John Baker says, "The best change is self-administered, and it is called innovation." John's inspirational message is an ideal kickoff or finale at your client event. Drive client loyalty and stimulate growth by having your clients adopt the five principles of *READY Thinking* right alongside you.

- Align *READY Thinking* with your corporate culture and achieve breakthrough results throughout your organization by using the READY Thinking Training Program™. This multimedia system is designed to be used by in-house facilitators to universally implement themes and techniques across your entire company, producing both unifying language and collective action. Get your organization "READY MADE" certified!

- Provide copies of *READY Thinking—Primed for Change* for client premiums, employee recognition, marketing incentives, or sales promotions.

For more information, go to **http://www.READYThinking.com** and share the gift of *READY Thinking*.

A note from John:

> *I've witnessed firsthand the benefits of empowering people with the skills of* READY Thinking. *All* READY Thinking *programs—from my keynote speeches to the full training curriculum—are delivered in an entertaining, engaging, and energetic way and are designed to be both fun and valuable for you, your organization, and your clients."*

—John

To Order Additional Copies of This Book

To order additional copies of *READY Thinking* please go to www.READYTHINKING.com